Business Processes and Procedures Necessary for a Successful Dental Career

Business Processes and Procedures Necessary for a Successful Dental Career

What You Need to Know Before You Graduate From Dental School

Kevin Coughlin DMD, MBA, MAGD

ISBN: 153284607X
ISBN 13: 9781532846076
Library of Congress Control Number: 2016906947
CreateSpace Independent Publishing Platform
North Charleston, South Carolina

I dedicate this book to my mother, my father, my wife, and my family, who taught me everything I need to know about managing and leading a successful business with determination, drive, hard work, honesty, and integrity, and who have never doubted me and have continually supported my love for this profession. I also dedicate this book to my team at Baystate Dental PC—it will always be your employees, your team members, who will ultimately make you and your practice successful. When your core group believes, likes, and trusts you and your judgment, you will achieve success. I also dedicate this book to Craig Abramowitz—you taught me everything I should *never do* in creating a successful team and business. Let's get going.

Business Processes and Procedures Necessary for a Successful Dental Career
I am a general dentist who has been practicing general dentistry every day and managing my dental business since 1983. Managing fourteen dental practices in Western Massachusetts, with over 150 employees, I have gained experience and have learned many things the hard way, like so many of my colleagues. I have elected to put together a textbook to help new graduates and practicing dentists who need a reference that is straightforward and easy to read, cutting through the red tape and providing knowledge to help others avoid mistakes that cost money, time, and stress.

Kevin Coughlin

About the Author

D r. Kevin Coughlin has a master's degree from the Academy of General Dentistry, a master's in health-care management from Western New England University, and a DMD from Tufts School of Dental Medicine. He has been teaching an elective practice-management course at Tufts since 2006. He has written several articles for *Excellence In Dentistry* and has published two books: *Your Tooth Is Killing Me: The Balance between the Clinical Aspect of Dentistry and the Business of Dentistry* and *Just Enough to Be Great in Your Dental Profession: Processes and Procedures for Success.*

CONTENTS

PREFACE

In the course of practicing dentistry, running a dental business, and teaching and writing about dentistry, I have come across some consistent findings. Recently graduated dentists are neither prepared to purchase and or manage a dental practice, nor do they know how to make informed decisions about basic business. There are several reasons for this; however, most dental schools are focused on teaching medicine and dentistry and all the clinical aspects that go along with being a health-care provider. I have also noted that the majority of dentists whom I have communicated with over the years have never taken any business courses. The majority of their time has been spent studying the sciences. Unfortunately, with the average debt from education at an estimated $220,000 and 30 percent of the students with debt over $300,000, it is critical for their well-being—and, in my opinion, the general success of our profession—that basic business and practice-management skills should be taught. I hope this book is the first step toward many long and successful careers.

CHAPTER 1

EMPLOYMENT OPTIONS

S tarting twelve months before your graduation from dental school, you should begin to give serious thought to how you would like to start your career. For most of you, this will be decided based on your personality and financial position. You may want to consider undertaking specialty training, entering a residency program or an associateship, starting your own practice, or buying an existing practice. You also might consider a career in public health or research, or working for an insurance company, the government, or a nonprofit. Consider all your options and weigh the risks, benefits, and alternatives of each.

You should also consider locations. What works best for you and your partner? Do you prefer the city or the country? Do you prefer a suburban lifestyle? You must also understand your debt structure and monthly expenses. Can you continue to postpone your debt? What will your monthly expenses be? What income will be necessary for you to earn in order to support yourself and perhaps your family? When you have addressed and answered those questions, remember that change is not a bad thing. It can be a great learning experience; however, it can be expensive and time consuming.

Remember, better decisions lead to better outcomes, and when it comes to business, the time value of money may be the most important concept for you to understand. The more money you put away as savings or investment and the sooner you do it, the better. It will provide you with the financial freedom that most individuals want. You can now work in your profession because you want to, not because you financially need to.

The vast majority of you will become dental associates, and you will have three options. You can start with a solo practice, a group practice, or some type of DSO (dental service organization). Let's start with joining a solo practice or a group practice owned and operated by a dentist. What most employers are looking for is drive, determination, and a willingness to stick it out when things get tough.

First, you must do your homework. Consider using your dental school's alumni to help you network; consider your own dentist as a source of networking; and consider placement centers such as Dental Career Network, Dentaljobs.org, Dental Workers, Monster.com, and Nationwide Dental Opportunities, as well as supply companies such as Patterson Dental and Henry Schein Dental Supply Company. While you are doing your research, you should have your CV and cover letter ready. Although many may disagree, I suggest including a picture of yourself as a way to stand out from the crowd.

Once this is completed, the next step is sending your CV out to the interested parties, which you have obtained from any of the above leads, and prepare for the phone interviews. Keep in mind sending your CV to all dentists in the location that interests you certainly does not do any harm. Allow at least thirty minutes for an interview, and schedule it for after clinical hours so neither of you feels pressured for time. Prepare a set of questions:

- Is the prospective employer looking for a full-time or part-time associate?
- Is there an expected length of association—one, two, three years, or longer?
- What are the employer's short- and long-term plans for the practice?
- Is the plan to find an associate who will move on, buy in, or buy out?
- How many square feet is the office? I suggest at least 2,500 square feet.

- How many dental treatment rooms are there? I suggest at least five.
- How many employees does the practice have? Who will be handling billing and collections? I suggest at least two receptionists, two certified dental assistants, and one full-time dental hygienist.
- How long have these employees been with the practice?
- How many previous dental associates has the practice had? Why did they leave?
- How many years has the practice been in business?
- What types of procedures does the practice do, and how many of these procedures are done annually?
- What are the top five clinical procedures done every year?
- What is the average number of new patients each month? I suggest at least thirty new patients every month to support one dentist.
- Where are these patients coming from? The best referral source is word of mouth.
- How many active patients, who have been in the practice for treatment at least once in the last eighteen months, are there? You need at least eighteen hundred active patients to support one dentist.
- How many patients are fee-for-service, and how many are insurance patients?
- What type of insurance is accepted? Are you able to balance-bill your dental-insurance patients? If so, at a discounted rate or your reasonable and customary rate?
- Does the practice have a marketing plan? What is it?
- Where are the new patients coming from? Why?
- How many patients are leaving per month?
- What are the gross and net production figures? Gross and net collection? What are the accounts receivable for thirty, sixty, and ninety days? You should be familiar with the rule of forty-five days. Accounts receivable should be forty-five days. That is, if the practice's net is $100,000 per month, then the receivables should be around $150,000.

- How much is dental-hygiene production and collection? It should be about 25 percent of the total practice revenue.
- Is the real estate owned or leased? If leased, what are the terms?
- Is there enough parking? There should be at least six parking spaces for every thousand square feet of office space, and the parking should be well lit.

The next step is a face-to-face interview. You should consider a full day, if possible, with part of the day as a working interview and the other part talking to team members. You should observe how the dentist interacts with patients and employees. You should observe equipment, the condition of the equipment, and sterilization procedures. What types of supplies are used? Where are they kept? If possible, spend time with the owner out of the office for lunch, dinner, or a coffee. Observe how he or she communicates and interacts. This face-to-face interview can show you a lot if you're interested. And you should be.

If both parties are interested, ask for a letter of intent and a professional service agreement or contract for your review. This professional service agreement should include

- a notice of engagement;
- start date;
- finish date;
- a list of duties;
- a list of qualifications and requirements;
- company guidelines; and
- a breakdown of compensation, the possibility of bonuses, and benefits.

It should address what happens in case of death, disability, or loss of license, and the process and procedures for resolution and disputes. It should address restrictive covenants, patient confidentiality, and compliance with federal and state laws and regulations. It should deal with outside interests or conflicts. It should also address eligibility to participate in insurance plans, billing assignments, and termination. What hours will you be working? What happens to accounts receivable? How many patients will you see every day? What type of insurance is accepted? Will you be working weekends and at night? Will you be on call? What is the buy-in price prior to you starting?

The ten mistakes I see dental associates make time and time again are as follows:

1. They start at the wrong job.
2. They take too long to leave that job.
3. They sign a poor employment agreement.
4. They do not understand the type of practice they are in and what is expected.
5. They leave the practice under bad terms.
6. They become too friendly with team members and patients.
7. They don't understand basic business.
8. They don't know how and when to refer.
9. They don't know how to market themselves.
10. They communicate poorly.

We should now discuss the processes and procedures associated with joining an MSO. Managed service organizations are growing and becoming part of the fabric of dental care in the United States. They have other names: dental service organizations (DSOs) and dental management service organizations (DMSOs). Whatever names these groups are called, it is critical that when applying to this type of organization, you ask the appropriate questions. The most important question is whether a private equity firm has involvement. If yes, to what degree? It will be critical in determining who is making the decisions. You should consider asking the following questions.

- Who is your employer?
- Who will be creating and editing your treatment plans?
- Who owns the dental professional entity?
- Who owns the management entity?
- What is the governance structure?
- Does the business entity have outside investors, and if so, who are they?

- Does the company have a managed service agreement? Does it comply with state law?
- What are the organization's expectations about productivity and patient volume?
- What is the dentist compensation formula, and how is the business entity involved?
- Who owns the leases?
- Who controls supplies and ordering?
- Who decides what dental lab is used?
- Who controls patient distribution?
- Who owns patient records? If you're terminated, will you have access?
- How is on-call handled?
- Who makes hiring and firing decisions?
- Will you be compliant with ADA Principles of Ethics and Code of Professional Conduct?
- Will you have access to all documentation and contracts that answer the above questions?
- Will you be able to buy in or purchase shares?

I suggest you consider asking for a guaranteed salary with provisions for quarterly bonuses. In most cases, you will be unfamiliar with the dental office and location, and your focus should be on quality of care and improving your skills, not worrying about meeting production or collection goals. I suggest you advocate for paid malpractice insurance, a stipend for continuing education, and personal and vacation time. In your second year, you should consider negotiating a percentage of net collected dollars produced by you. Typically this will be 32–40 percent, with you being personally responsible for 32–40 percent of your personal laboratory bill.

Starting your career on the right track may be one of the best business decisions you can make for yourself and—for your finances. Carefully consider all options. Do your homework. Make sure you factor in your short- and long-term goals.

My intent is not to influence you whether corporate dentistry is good or bad. It is to make sure you are fully informed and understand who is making the decisions and what the motives are.

CHAPTER 2

PLANNING YOUR CAREER

I s it even possible to plan your career? As a seasoned practitioner, I look back on my career, and I would like to say yes. However, many things just happen, and things have a way of working out. If you can stack the deck in your favor, why not?

In the previous chapter, we addressed different career paths. Any of them can be rewarding, but you should consider the following when planning your career. Start first with your personality—what drives and motivates you, what excites you, and what are you passionate about? After you answer those questions, bring into the equation your debt load and your desire and need for income. Next, think about what locations interest you: if you're a skier, perhaps the mountains; if you like the sun and water, perhaps the coast—you get my point? When you are starting out, you may not see the importance, but family ties might play a big part in your decision-making process. Being close to family has many advantages, particularly as you get older; perhaps family members will need assistance.

You should ask yourself these questions:

- Do you prefer to handpick your employees?
- Do you enjoy networking, and are you good at it?
- Do you have a clear vision of what you want your dental practice to be?
- Are you comfortable developing policies and procedures for a wide variety of topics?

- Are you passionate about your professional environment and surroundings?
- Are you willing to put in an enormous amount of time and energy to get something started?
- Are you willing to be financially frugal for a time?
- Are you willing to create your own patient base?
- Do you feel you are an entrepreneur?
- Do you have the skills to sell yourself, or are you willing to learn?
- Do you want a connection with the community?

If the answers to these questions are yes, then most likely you will only be happy being your own boss, so I strongly suggest you pursue that direction. Type A individuals and true entrepreneurs usually will be happiest being in charge and making decisions. Please think long and hard about this point, and make sure you really understand what you are getting into.

CHAPTER 3

UNDERSTANDING MACROECONOMICS

When people discuss economics, they are usually referring to macroeconomics, which is looking at the entire economy and the forces that affect it. Microeconomics looks at individual businesses and people and how they act toward changing conditions.

The law of supply and demand is about making choices. In a capitalist economy, people are free to make choices, or they should be. In communist and socialist societies, it has been predetermined how much of each product and service is provided and at what price. When economists talk about demand, they are really just referring to the quantity of goods or services that people are willing and able to buy at the given price. Supply, on the other hand, means the quantity of goods or services that suppliers are willing and able to offer at every possible price. In general, as demand for a product or service goes up, so does the price; similarly, as the demand goes down, so does the price.

There are many factors that can influence the laws of supply and demand, including

- the general prosperity of individuals as indicated by their disposable income;
- demographics such as educational level and number of wage earners;
- the number of producers and their productivity;

- technological improvements; and
- regulations.

Dentistry has many advantages that can improve your chances of being profitable. Currently, there are too few dentists available to provide services, owing to the limited number of dental schools, the limited number of graduates, and regulations by federal and state agencies that currently only allow licensed dentists to provide dental care and treatment. At present, it is not possible to farm out dental care to be performed by robots. Conversely, as government, insurance companies, and corporate dentistry get more involved, competition will increase, and the ability to provide fee-for-service treatment may be a thing of the past. What this means is that the dentist who is the most competitive and most efficient and effective in providing care and services will do the best.

Dentistry, like most of health care, appears to have less control over fee schedules, and this creates a much more difficult environment in which you can be profitable. I submit that the best business solution for dentists is the elimination of all dental insurance plans to allow the free market to work. This, of course, is an unrealistic expectation, so sharpen your skills and be prepared. I predict fewer dentists will enter the marketplace due to high education debt, lower income potential, and increased barriers to entry due to difficulty in competing with government health care, corporate dentistry, and nonprofit agencies. With that said, there will always be a group of patients and providers who will seek a higher level of service and care and be able to afford that service and care. However, you must be prepared to offer a truly unique approach to treatment and service combined with business acumen and marketing, or you will be destined to fail.

The gross domestic product (GDP) is the market value of all goods and services produced for a country. When GDP is increasing, the economy is growing, and when GDP is decreasing the economy is shrinking, or goods and services are diminishing or are in decline. GDP consists of four categories. The largest by far is domestic consumption, which is good for dentistry since individuals are willing to purchase your goods and services. However, there is a lot of competition for consumer or patient dollars. In my opinion, consumers decide to spend their limited financial resources on dental care for cosmetic reasons, fear, and pain. Cosmetic reasons are a huge motivator of consumers wanting to look and feel good about themselves. With regard to fear, most consumers are frightened about the effects of not receiving care and treatment. And pain, as all dentists know and understand, motivates consumers to demand care and treatment as soon as possible.

The next-largest category after domestic consumption is government spending. Third is investment in plant and equipment, and last are net exports. So GDP = C + I + G + NE, where C = consumption; I = investment; G = government spending; and NE = net exports. You should understand that business cycles are really nothing more than understanding that nothing stays the same. All businesses, like our economy, have peaks and valleys, and so will your practice. You must have the stomach and stick-to-itiveness to weather the downturns, and the discipline not to squander the upturns. Always have an emergency fund or line of working capital available so you can make the necessary changes to adapt to the business cycle.

Inflation is a general increase in the price of goods and services, and it is generally agreed that a 1–2 percent increase per year is acceptable. As a dentist, you not only need to increase your fees 1–2 percent to break even, but also you may want to raise fees beyond that to increase your profit. Otherwise, you will just continue to break even and not really be growing. Deflation is a decrease in the general price of goods and services; this only occurred in the United States during the Great Depression in the early 1930s.

Inflation is generally viewed by two economic measures: the consumer price index (CPI), which means the price of goods such as food, clothing, and energy, and the producer price index (PPI), which looks at the cost of raw materials and labor for producers.

How is inflation controlled? The government controls it, or tries to, through fiscal and monetary policy. Fiscal policy is the action of the federal government to try to manage the economy. This is done through Congress and the president. Congress passes legislation, and the president signs it into law. The tools available to accomplish this include changes in tax laws, increasing or decreasing government spending, and financing deficits through borrowing by issuing new government securities. Fiscal policy, in general, attempts to maintain full employment, keep prices stable, and continue to have GDP growth. These are lofty goals, like finding the perfect partner to marry! Do they really exist?

Monetary policy [H1]

Monetary policy is controlled by the Federal Reserve Board, which should act independently to implement decisions. The Federal Reserve has the ability to change reserve requirements for banks and the discount rate that banks charge their customers. The discount rate is the rate charged to banks to borrow money to issue loans. By having this power and control, in essence, the Federal Reserve has the ability to encourage or discourage banks from lending money, and this can affect stock and bond prices. The Federal Reserve conducts open-market operations and is composed of a board of governors referred to as the FOMC (Federal Open Market Committee) and twelve Federal Reserve district banks. The Federal Reserve issues money and makes loans to commercial banks, who then lend money to businesses and individuals. Some actions that the Federal Reserve uses to accomplish its goal of creating noninflationary growth in GDP are purchasing government securities, lowering reserve requirements, lowering the discount rate, selling government securities, increasing reserve requirements, or raising the discount rate.

CHAPTER 4

MANAGING YOUR MONEY

Of all the information provided to improve your financial security, the information in this chapter may offer you the best chance
of success. What I am suggesting is coming up with a financial
plan to provide you with financial freedom in order to work and pursue
your career because you want to, rather than because you need to. The
goal includes planning for emergencies, understanding and balancing
your spending, and increasing your net worth. Increasing net worth is
just increasing your assets and decreasing your liabilities, and under normal circumstance, this should occur in the normal progression of time.

During your career, most of you will acquire more assets and see
your liabilities decrease. The real trick is to speed this process up, so the
time value of your money is increased. In my opinion, the questions that
always loom are these: What is the correct amount of net worth? In other
words, what should my goal be? And how do I know what that number is?

Whatever yearly income you feel you can live comfortably on, multiply that number by twelve. If you can live comfortably on $150,000 per
year, your target number should be $1.8 million. The biggest obstacle in
achieving this goal is the inability to control spending. You really only
have two choices: either spend your money or save it. Consider a goal of
saving 10–20 percent of after-tax dollars each and every year—when possible, save more. Most importantly, the earlier you do this, the better the
financial picture for you and your family due to the time value of money.
Last, prepare for life's unexpected twists and turns, the emergencies that
happen in all lives. For this, I suggest a separate account holding enough

money to allow you to pay your expenses for six to nine months. So if your expenses are $5,000 per month, you should set aside between $30,000 and $45,000. You should be doing this not only for your personal finances but also for your business if you're self-employed. The tools available to accomplish these goals are money management, insurance, retirement plans, understanding and controlling your taxes, and estate planning. Consider assembling a team to help you since very few can do this on their own. I suggest an accountant (CPA) who is an expert in taxes; a certified financial planner (CFP) who has been properly vetted and truly understands your goals and financial picture; a lending institution that specializes in small businesses and can also address your personal needs; an attorney who also specializes in professional corporations, estate planning, and litigation; an investment group who, again, has been fully vetted and understands your assets and liabilities; and an insurance group who can handle personal and business insurance for you and your family. This team is critical to your success and the success of your team members in your dental office. It is critical that the group you assemble is working together, not independently, so all parties involved know what the others are doing and are working toward the common goal of establishing your financial success and freedom.

CHAPTER 5

INSURANCE

There is almost nothing I enjoy less than insurance; however, it is a part of life today, and it's necessary to understand and control it, if possible. In general, I suggest always going with the highest deductible and only purchasing the insurance you absolutely need.

Most of you reading this will need personal and business insurance. Both are necessary, and each is different, but the goal is the same in both instances: reduce your risk and exposure to the four Ds—death, disability, divorce, and dissolution. The real trick is determining what the right balance is for you, your family, and your practice so you are not over- or underinsured. Your insurance needs should be updated every three to five years, when a life-changing event occurs, or if your financial picture changes significantly.

On the personal side, you should consider life, homeowners, and personal excess liability, automobile, disability, medical, and hospitalization insurance. On the business side, you should consider workers' compensation, unemployment compensation, Social Security, office overhead, loss of use, business liability, malpractice, medical care expenses, loss of income, premature death, excess liability, or umbrella insurances. As you review your insurance options and plans that are available to you, ask about tax consequences, features of the plans, risk management, limitations, benefits, purposes, and types available to you, your family, and business. These are critical questions, and the better you understand the answers, the greater the likelihood you will be pleased with your decisions. But if you can afford the losses, in almost all cases you will be financially better off without that policy, and you can save the premium dollars.

Medical insurance has four general parts. Basic coverage insures against losses from common medical costs such as office and ER visits, minor hospital stays, prescription drugs, and in some cases, high-frequency, low-cost procedures. Since this insurance pays for many types of care that occur frequently, it tends to be costly. Major medical really comes into play where basic coverage stops. It helps with major hospitalizations and, in general, has a total lifetime benefit of $1–2 million. Excess major medical occurs when major medical no longer provides coverage and in general is not that expensive to purchase. Last, you have comprehensive insurance, which provides coverage for all of the above. By bundling them, they can provide better coverage, with less chance of missing something and perhaps at a lower cost.

As you evaluate your medical insurance, you should review the deductible policy—the amount the insured has to pay out of pocket. In general, the higher the deductible, the lower the cost of coverage. Copayment means that you, as the insured, pay part of the cost; in other words, you have skin in the game and may be a more discerning consumer. In most cases, copay will be 20 percent. Limitations are important to understand because some items, such as certain treatments or drugs, will be excluded from coverage. The network provider concept is also important to understand since your coverage may be limited only to those providers who are in network. This can reduce your cost and out-of-pocket expenses but may limit your choice. Finally, utilization reviews may require you to receive second opinions before treatment is started.

You will most likely need disability income insurance more than life insurance. In real terms, you are much more likely to need disability insurance while working, and the average length of disability is thirteen months if it occurs. In most cases, disability insurance only pays about 66–75 percent of your lost income.

You should also consider the tax consequences of how these plans are paid. In general, if your business is paying the premium, then the dollars received will be taxed; however, if you pay for the insurance yourself, then you can receive the benefits tax-free. Before a plan is purchased, you will need to verify your income. You will probably not be able to get personal disability insurance in amounts greater than your current income. You should also make sure that the plan allows cost-of-living adjustments (COLA) in the future and adjustments allowed as your income increases.

Plans often carry exclusions for self-inflicted injuries such as unsuccessful suicide, illegal drug use, injuries as a result of war, and preexisting conditions. You should consider not only the amount of monthly benefits but also the length of time of the elimination period. In most cases, the longer you wait for the benefit to start, the less expensive the premium. Typically, people choose a waiting period of 30–365 days. Next, you need to determine the length of the benefit payment. Again, the longer you choose to be paid the benefit, the more expensive the premium. In most cases, you will be getting a plan that will pay up to the age of sixty-five. As you age, you should review this coverage. You may want to consider eliminating it to save the premium dollars toward your retirement. You should also review the policy to make sure you have clauses that allow renewability and state that the insurance cannot be canceled. Another important point is a guaranteed purchase option so if you need more insurance, you can get it.

Last, and in my view, perhaps most important, be sure you understand the type of disability insurance you are purchasing. One type of plan, called an "own occupation" policy, means it will pay you if you cannot perform the duties of a dentist. A less expensive type of disability plan is called an "any occupation" policy, in which case, if you were able to do some type of job other than dentistry, the plan might not pay. I suggest you consider the own occupation plan.

Life insurance can be used for estate planning, for cross-purchase buy-sell agreements—a vehicle that banks may require for collateral on debt—and to provide money to your family, friends, or estate to pay debts or leave money for future generations. Some options you might consider include term insurance, which is only in effect for a certain period of time. In most cases you cannot borrow against this type of life insurance, and it will not accumulate any cash value. Whole life insurance can last for your whole life. Some of your premium dollars act like a term life plan, and the other part of your premium provides cash value that can accumulate over time. In general, this latter type of life insurance is more expensive and is more profitable to insurance agents because of a higher commission. You may also have an option of purchasing a hybrid type of life insurance, with traits similar to a term plan but with cash value and investment options. Variable life insurance policies take the savings portion of a whole life policy and invest in other vehicles, which may give you a better return than a typical whole life plan. Universal life insurance is also similar to a whole life plan; however, it pays you a competitive interest rate. Finally, you have endowment life insurance, which will pay you a dividend on a regular timetable. If your goal is to buy life insurance to provide your family income, consider purchasing an amount that is equal to eight times your annual income. Another decision you must make is who your beneficiary will be, which simply means who will get the money from the plan. This should be spelled out clearly in your plan and in your will. Please keep in mind that if this is done incorrectly, these funds could be tied up in court for years and also have enormous tax consequences for the estate.

Auto insurance is made up of parts A, B, C, and D. Part A is liability coverage when you are the cause of an accident. Part B provides medical payments to the policyholder or anyone else in the car with you. Part C helps you when an accident occurs, and the other party is uninsured and is the cause of the accident. Part D provides coverage to the damaged vehicle that is covered under the policy. Comprehensive coverage includes payment to damage not caused by a collision, such as damaged wheel wells or a cracked windshield. Collision coverage provides repair to the policyholder's car that is damaged in a collision. And always remember—your personal automobile insurance does not provide coverage if an employee is using your car for company business.

Homeowner's insurance has two basic jobs: to protect the policyholder against loss of property and to protect the policyholder against liability that arises from owning the property. Property coverage includes the dwelling, other structures, personal property, and loss of use. Liability coverage under a homeowner's policy includes personal liability, medical payments to others, and damage to property of others. In general, there are seven types of homeowner's insurance:

1. Basic includes fire, lightning, extended coverage, vandalism, theft, glass breakage, personal contents, and personal liability.
2. Comprehensive includes basic and almost any other type or cause.
3. All risk is really all causes unless specifically excluded from the coverage.
4. Personal property is mostly for tenants.
5. All risk is on building and personal property.
6. Personal property and loss of use coverage is for condominium unit owners.
7. The last type of coverage is for buildings and personal property and is more limited than basic and generally for buildings and homes that may not meet underwriting requirements.

Umbrella liability insurance or personal excess liability insurance should be considered carefully. It provides extra coverage when needed to protect your personal assets. This type of plan may provide an additional $1–2 million in coverage. Since these types of plans are relatively inexpensive, many experts suggest purchasing one, and they may be correct. In my experience, when attorneys see extra coverage, it provides extra incentive. Please do not take this comment out of context; however, it is something to consider when you evaluate this and any other type of liability insurance.

There are some additional points to consider. Insurance premiums that are for business purposes are a cost of doing business and are for the most part tax deductible. Insurance premiums that are for personal use are generally not tax deductible. Sometimes people pay for disability insurance premiums themselves, so if needed, the benefits are tax-free, and if not needed, they will bonus themselves out to pay the premium cost. Life insurance benefits are tax-free; however, the premiums that are paid are not tax deductible.

Under insurances, you should also be familiar with health savings accounts (HSAs). An HSA is an important vehicle to have in your business, or as an employee, since medical insurance will be one of your biggest expenses. In basic terms, you are able to put away pretax dollars in an HSA account to help pay for deductibles, copays, and other costs that your medical plan may not cover. In some cases, the plan is written so that if you do not use it, you lose it; in other cases, if you do not use it, it gets rolled over into the next year and can act almost as another savings account.

CHAPTER 6

UNDERSTANDING BUSINESS FINANCE

The most important concept in finance is determining the value of money over time. Money you have today is more valuable than money in the future. Most people would rather have the money today. The interest rate is really what determines how important this is. The higher your interest rate and the longer the time your dollars have to compound, the better your financial picture will be in the future. Your largest asset will probably be your dental practice; however, most will sell at the end of their careers, and the time those dollars have to grow and compound is usually short. This has to weigh against the fact that when you do sell, your income will probably decrease, so consider your options carefully.

The future value of a present amount is the future amount of an initial deposit when compounded for a given amount of time. In order to determine that, you use the financial calculator or a Future Value of a Single Present Amount Table and put in the following information:

PV = present value, or the amount in today's dollars
I = interest rate for each period compounded
N = the number of periods or years of compounding
FV = future value

Future Value Factor for a Single Present Amount
(Interest rate = r, Number of periods = n)

n\r	1%	2%	3%	4%	5%	6%	7%	8%	9%	10%	11%	12%	13%	14%	15%	16%	17%
1	1.0100	1.0200	1.0300	1.0400	1.0500	1.0600	1.0700	1.0800	1.0900	1.1000	1.1100	1.1200	1.1300	1.1400	1.1500	1.1600	1.1700
2	1.0201	1.0404	1.0609	1.0816	1.1025	1.1236	1.1449	1.1664	1.1881	1.2100	1.2321	1.2544	1.2769	1.2996	1.3225	1.3456	1.3689
3	1.0303	1.0612	1.0927	1.1249	1.1576	1.1910	1.2250	1.2597	1.2950	1.3310	1.3676	1.4049	1.4429	1.4815	1.5209	1.5609	1.6016
4	1.0406	1.0824	1.1255	1.1699	1.2155	1.2625	1.3108	1.3605	1.4116	1.4641	1.5181	1.5735	1.6305	1.6890	1.7490	1.8106	1.8739
5	1.0510	1.1041	1.1593	1.2167	1.2763	1.3382	1.4026	1.4693	1.5386	1.6105	1.6851	1.7623	1.8424	1.9254	2.0114	2.1003	2.1924
6	1.0615	1.1262	1.1941	1.2653	1.3401	1.4185	1.5007	1.5869	1.6771	1.7716	1.8704	1.9738	2.0820	2.1950	2.3131	2.4364	2.5652
7	1.0721	1.1487	1.2299	1.3159	1.4071	1.5036	1.6058	1.7138	1.8280	1.9487	2.0762	2.2107	2.3526	2.5023	2.6600	2.8262	3.0012
8	1.0829	1.1717	1.2668	1.3686	1.4775	1.5938	1.7182	1.8509	1.9926	2.1436	2.3045	2.4760	2.6584	2.8526	3.0590	3.2784	3.5115
9	1.0937	1.1951	1.3048	1.4233	1.5513	1.6895	1.8385	1.9990	2.1719	2.3579	2.5580	2.7731	3.0040	3.2519	3.5179	3.8030	4.1084
10	1.1046	1.2190	1.3439	1.4802	1.6289	1.7908	1.9672	2.1589	2.3674	2.5937	2.8394	3.1058	3.3946	3.7072	4.0456	4.4114	4.8068
11	1.1157	1.2434	1.3842	1.5395	1.7103	1.8983	2.1049	2.3316	2.5804	2.8531	3.1518	3.4785	3.8359	4.2262	4.6524	5.1173	5.6240
12	1.1268	1.2682	1.4258	1.6010	1.7959	2.0122	2.2522	2.5182	2.8127	3.1384	3.4985	3.8960	4.3345	4.8179	5.3503	5.9360	6.5801
13	1.1381	1.2936	1.4685	1.6651	1.8856	2.1329	2.4098	2.7196	3.0658	3.4523	3.8833	4.3635	4.8980	5.4924	6.1528	6.8858	7.6987
14	1.1495	1.3195	1.5126	1.7317	1.9799	2.2609	2.5785	2.9372	3.3417	3.7975	4.3104	4.8871	5.5348	6.2613	7.0757	7.9875	9.0075
15	1.1610	1.3459	1.5580	1.8009	2.0789	2.3966	2.7590	3.1722	3.6425	4.1772	4.7846	5.4736	6.2543	7.1379	8.1371	9.2655	10.5387
16	1.1726	1.3728	1.6047	1.8730	2.1829	2.5404	2.9522	3.4259	3.9703	4.5950	5.3109	6.1304	7.0673	8.1372	9.3576	10.7480	12.3303
17	1.1843	1.4002	1.6528	1.9479	2.2920	2.6928	3.1588	3.7000	4.3276	5.0545	5.8951	6.8660	7.9861	9.2765	10.7613	12.4677	14.4265
18	1.1961	1.4282	1.7024	2.0258	2.4066	2.8543	3.3799	3.9960	4.7171	5.5599	6.5436	7.6900	9.0243	10.5752	12.3755	14.4625	16.8790
19	1.2081	1.4568	1.7535	2.1068	2.5270	3.0256	3.6165	4.3157	5.1417	6.1159	7.2633	8.6128	10.1974	12.0557	14.2318	16.7765	19.7484
20	1.2202	1.4859	1.8061	2.1911	2.6533	3.2071	3.8697	4.6610	5.6044	6.7275	8.0623	9.6463	11.5231	13.7435	16.3665	19.4608	23.1056
21	1.2324	1.5157	1.8603	2.2788	2.7860	3.3996	4.1406	5.0338	6.1088	7.4002	8.9492	10.8038	13.0211	15.6676	18.8215	22.5745	27.0336
22	1.2447	1.5460	1.9161	2.3699	2.9253	3.6035	4.4304	5.4365	6.6586	8.1403	9.9336	12.1003	14.7138	17.8610	21.6447	26.1864	31.6293
23	1.2572	1.5769	1.9736	2.4647	3.0715	3.8197	4.7405	5.8715	7.2579	8.9543	11.0263	13.5523	16.6266	20.3616	24.8915	30.3762	37.0062
24	1.2697	1.6084	2.0328	2.5633	3.2251	4.0489	5.0724	6.3412	7.9111	9.8497	12.2392	15.1786	18.7881	23.2122	28.6252	35.2364	43.2973
25	1.2824	1.6406	2.0938	2.6658	3.3864	4.2919	5.4274	6.8485	8.6231	10.8347	13.5855	17.0001	21.2305	26.4619	32.9190	40.8742	50.6578
26	1.2953	1.6734	2.1566	2.7725	3.5557	4.5494	5.8074	7.3964	9.3992	11.9182	15.0799	19.0401	23.9905	30.1666	37.8568	47.4141	59.2697
27	1.3082	1.7069	2.2213	2.8834	3.7335	4.8223	6.2139	7.9881	10.2451	13.1100	16.7386	21.3249	27.1093	34.3899	43.5353	55.0004	69.3455
28	1.3213	1.7410	2.2879	2.9987	3.9201	5.1117	6.6488	8.6271	11.1671	14.4210	18.5799	23.8839	30.6335	39.2045	50.0656	63.8004	81.1342
29	1.3345	1.7758	2.3566	3.1187	4.1161	5.4184	7.1143	9.3173	12.1722	15.8631	20.6237	26.7499	34.6158	44.6931	57.5755	74.0085	94.9271
30	1.3478	1.8114	2.4273	3.2434	4.3219	5.7435	7.6123	10.0627	13.2677	17.4494	22.8923	29.9599	39.1159	50.9502	66.2118	85.8499	111.0647
31	1.3613	1.8476	2.5001	3.3731	4.5380	6.0881	8.1451	10.8677	14.4618	19.1943	25.4104	33.5551	44.2010	58.0832	76.1435	99.5859	129.9456
32	1.3749	1.8845	2.5751	3.5081	4.7649	6.4534	8.7153	11.7371	15.7633	21.1138	28.2056	37.5817	49.9471	66.2148	87.5651	115.5196	152.0364
33	1.3887	1.9222	2.6523	3.6484	5.0032	6.8406	9.3253	12.6760	17.1820	23.2252	31.3082	42.0915	56.4402	75.4849	100.6998	134.0027	177.8826
34	1.4026	1.9607	2.7319	3.7943	5.2533	7.2510	9.9781	13.6901	18.7284	25.5477	34.7521	47.1425	63.7774	86.0528	115.8048	155.4432	208.1226
35	1.4166	1.9999	2.8139	3.9461	5.5160	7.6861	10.6766	14.7853	20.4140	28.1024	38.5749	52.7996	72.0685	98.1002	133.1755	180.3141	243.5035
36	1.4308	2.0399	2.8983	4.1039	5.7918	8.1473	11.4239	15.9682	22.2512	30.9127	42.8181	59.1356	81.4374	111.8342	153.1519	209.1643	284.8991
37	1.4451	2.0807	2.9852	4.2681	6.0814	8.6361	12.2236	17.2456	24.2538	34.0039	47.5281	66.2318	92.0243	127.4910	176.1246	242.6306	333.3319
38	1.4595	2.1223	3.0748	4.4388	6.3855	9.1543	13.0793	18.6253	26.4367	37.4043	52.7562	74.1797	103.9874	145.3397	202.5433	281.4515	389.9983
39	1.4741	2.1647	3.1670	4.6164	6.7048	9.7035	13.9948	20.1153	28.8160	41.1448	58.5593	83.0812	117.5059	165.6873	232.9248	326.4838	456.2980
40	1.4889	2.2080	3.2620	4.8010	7.0400	10.2857	14.9745	21.7245	31.4094	45.2593	65.0009	93.0510	132.7816	188.8835	267.8635	378.7212	533.8687
41	1.5038	2.2522	3.3599	4.9931	7.3920	10.9029	16.0227	23.4625	34.2363	49.7852	72.1510	104.2177	150.0432	215.3272	308.0431	439.3165	624.6264
42	1.5188	2.2972	3.4607	5.1928	7.7616	11.5570	17.1443	25.3395	37.3175	54.7637	80.0876	116.7231	169.5488	245.4730	354.2496	509.6072	730.8129
43	1.5340	2.3432	3.5645	5.4005	8.1497	12.2505	18.3444	27.3666	40.6761	60.2401	88.8972	130.7299	191.5907	279.8392	407.3870	591.1443	855.0511
44	1.5493	2.3901	3.6715	5.6165	8.5572	12.9855	19.6285	29.5560	44.3370	66.2641	98.6759	146.4175	216.4968	319.0167	468.4950	685.7274	1000.410
45	1.5648	2.4379	3.7816	5.8412	8.9850	13.7646	21.0025	31.9204	48.3273	72.8905	109.5302	163.9876	244.6414	363.6791	538.7693	795.4438	1170.479

This calculation can help you figure out how to plan for future expenditures or savings. Consider the following example. You would like to invest $5,000 in a CD, earning 4 percent interest compounded annually, and you want to know what the CD will be worth in ten years.

Present Value Factor for a Single Future Amount
(Interest rate = r, Number of periods = n)

n\r	1%	2%	3%	4%	5%	6%	7%	8%	9%	10%	11%	12%	13%	14%	15%	16%	17%
1	0.9901	0.9804	0.9709	0.9615	0.9524	0.9434	0.9346	0.9259	0.9174	0.9091	0.9009	0.8929	0.8850	0.8772	0.8696	0.8621	0.8547
2	0.9803	0.9612	0.9426	0.9246	0.9070	0.8900	0.8734	0.8573	0.8417	0.8264	0.8116	0.7972	0.7831	0.7695	0.7561	0.7432	0.7305
3	0.9706	0.9423	0.9151	0.8890	0.8638	0.8396	0.8163	0.7938	0.7722	0.7513	0.7312	0.7118	0.6931	0.6750	0.6575	0.6407	0.6244
4	0.9610	0.9238	0.8885	0.8548	0.8227	0.7921	0.7629	0.7350	0.7084	0.6830	0.6587	0.6355	0.6133	0.5921	0.5718	0.5523	0.5337
5	0.9515	0.9057	0.8626	0.8219	0.7835	0.7473	0.7130	0.6806	0.6499	0.6209	0.5935	0.5674	0.5428	0.5194	0.4972	0.4761	0.4561
6	0.9420	0.8880	0.8375	0.7903	0.7462	0.7050	0.6663	0.6302	0.5963	0.5645	0.5346	0.5066	0.4803	0.4556	0.4323	0.4104	0.3898
7	0.9327	0.8706	0.8131	0.7599	0.7107	0.6651	0.6227	0.5835	0.5470	0.5132	0.4817	0.4523	0.4251	0.3996	0.3759	0.3538	0.3332
8	0.9235	0.8535	0.7894	0.7307	0.6768	0.6274	0.5820	0.5403	0.5019	0.4665	0.4339	0.4039	0.3762	0.3506	0.3269	0.3050	0.2848
9	0.9143	0.8368	0.7664	0.7026	0.6446	0.5919	0.5439	0.5002	0.4604	0.4241	0.3909	0.3606	0.3329	0.3075	0.2843	0.2630	0.2434
10	0.9053	0.8203	0.7441	0.6756	0.6139	0.5584	0.5083	0.4632	0.4224	0.3855	0.3522	0.3220	0.2946	0.2697	0.2472	0.2267	0.2080
11	0.8963	0.8043	0.7224	0.6496	0.5847	0.5268	0.4751	0.4289	0.3875	0.3505	0.3173	0.2875	0.2607	0.2366	0.2149	0.1954	0.1778
12	0.8874	0.7885	0.7014	0.6246	0.5568	0.4970	0.4440	0.3971	0.3555	0.3186	0.2858	0.2567	0.2307	0.2076	0.1869	0.1685	0.1520
13	0.8787	0.7730	0.6810	0.6006	0.5303	0.4688	0.4150	0.3677	0.3262	0.2897	0.2575	0.2292	0.2042	0.1821	0.1625	0.1452	0.1299
14	0.8700	0.7579	0.6611	0.5775	0.5051	0.4423	0.3878	0.3405	0.2992	0.2633	0.2320	0.2046	0.1807	0.1597	0.1413	0.1252	0.1110
15	0.8613	0.7430	0.6419	0.5553	0.4810	0.4173	0.3624	0.3152	0.2745	0.2394	0.2090	0.1827	0.1599	0.1401	0.1229	0.1079	0.0949
16	0.8528	0.7284	0.6232	0.5339	0.4581	0.3936	0.3387	0.2919	0.2519	0.2176	0.1883	0.1631	0.1415	0.1229	0.1069	0.0930	0.0811
17	0.8444	0.7142	0.6050	0.5134	0.4363	0.3714	0.3166	0.2703	0.2311	0.1978	0.1696	0.1456	0.1252	0.1078	0.0929	0.0802	0.0693
18	0.8360	0.7002	0.5874	0.4936	0.4155	0.3503	0.2959	0.2502	0.2120	0.1799	0.1528	0.1300	0.1108	0.0946	0.0808	0.0691	0.0592
19	0.8277	0.6864	0.5703	0.4746	0.3957	0.3305	0.2765	0.2317	0.1945	0.1635	0.1377	0.1161	0.0981	0.0829	0.0703	0.0596	0.0506
20	0.8195	0.6730	0.5537	0.4564	0.3769	0.3118	0.2584	0.2145	0.1784	0.1486	0.1240	0.1037	0.0868	0.0728	0.0611	0.0514	0.0433
21	0.8114	0.6598	0.5375	0.4388	0.3589	0.2942	0.2415	0.1987	0.1637	0.1351	0.1117	0.0926	0.0768	0.0638	0.0531	0.0443	0.0370
22	0.8034	0.6468	0.5219	0.4220	0.3418	0.2775	0.2257	0.1839	0.1502	0.1228	0.1007	0.0826	0.0680	0.0560	0.0462	0.0382	0.0316
23	0.7954	0.6342	0.5067	0.4057	0.3256	0.2618	0.2109	0.1703	0.1378	0.1117	0.0907	0.0738	0.0601	0.0491	0.0402	0.0329	0.0270
24	0.7876	0.6217	0.4919	0.3901	0.3101	0.2470	0.1971	0.1577	0.1264	0.1015	0.0817	0.0659	0.0532	0.0431	0.0349	0.0284	0.0231
25	0.7798	0.6095	0.4776	0.3751	0.2953	0.2330	0.1842	0.1460	0.1160	0.0923	0.0736	0.0588	0.0471	0.0378	0.0304	0.0245	0.0197
26	0.7720	0.5976	0.4637	0.3607	0.2812	0.2198	0.1722	0.1352	0.1064	0.0839	0.0663	0.0525	0.0417	0.0331	0.0264	0.0211	0.0169
27	0.7644	0.5859	0.4502	0.3468	0.2678	0.2074	0.1609	0.1252	0.0976	0.0763	0.0597	0.0469	0.0369	0.0291	0.0230	0.0182	0.0144
28	0.7568	0.5744	0.4371	0.3335	0.2551	0.1956	0.1504	0.1159	0.0895	0.0693	0.0538	0.0419	0.0326	0.0255	0.0200	0.0157	0.0123
29	0.7493	0.5631	0.4243	0.3207	0.2429	0.1846	0.1406	0.1073	0.0822	0.0630	0.0485	0.0374	0.0289	0.0224	0.0174	0.0135	0.0105
30	0.7419	0.5521	0.4120	0.3083	0.2314	0.1741	0.1314	0.0994	0.0754	0.0573	0.0437	0.0334	0.0256	0.0196	0.0151	0.0116	0.0090
31	0.7346	0.5412	0.4000	0.2965	0.2204	0.1643	0.1228	0.0920	0.0691	0.0521	0.0394	0.0298	0.0226	0.0172	0.0131	0.0100	0.0077
32	0.7273	0.5306	0.3883	0.2851	0.2099	0.1550	0.1147	0.0852	0.0634	0.0474	0.0355	0.0266	0.0200	0.0151	0.0114	0.0087	0.0066
33	0.7201	0.5202	0.3770	0.2741	0.1999	0.1462	0.1072	0.0789	0.0582	0.0431	0.0319	0.0238	0.0177	0.0132	0.0099	0.0075	0.0056
34	0.7130	0.5100	0.3660	0.2636	0.1904	0.1379	0.1002	0.0730	0.0534	0.0391	0.0288	0.0212	0.0157	0.0116	0.0086	0.0064	0.0048
35	0.7059	0.5000	0.3554	0.2534	0.1813	0.1301	0.0937	0.0676	0.0490	0.0356	0.0259	0.0189	0.0139	0.0102	0.0075	0.0055	0.0041
36	0.6989	0.4902	0.3450	0.2437	0.1727	0.1227	0.0875	0.0626	0.0449	0.0323	0.0234	0.0169	0.0123	0.0089	0.0065	0.0048	0.0035
37	0.6920	0.4806	0.3350	0.2343	0.1644	0.1158	0.0818	0.0580	0.0412	0.0294	0.0210	0.0151	0.0109	0.0078	0.0057	0.0041	0.0030
38	0.6852	0.4712	0.3252	0.2253	0.1566	0.1092	0.0765	0.0537	0.0378	0.0267	0.0190	0.0135	0.0096	0.0069	0.0049	0.0036	0.0026
39	0.6784	0.4619	0.3158	0.2166	0.1491	0.1031	0.0715	0.0497	0.0347	0.0243	0.0171	0.0120	0.0085	0.0060	0.0043	0.0031	0.0022
40	0.6717	0.4529	0.3066	0.2083	0.1420	0.0972	0.0668	0.0460	0.0318	0.0221	0.0154	0.0107	0.0075	0.0053	0.0037	0.0026	0.0019
41	0.6650	0.4440	0.2976	0.2003	0.1353	0.0917	0.0624	0.0426	0.0292	0.0201	0.0139	0.0096	0.0067	0.0046	0.0032	0.0023	0.0016
42	0.6584	0.4353	0.2890	0.1926	0.1288	0.0865	0.0583	0.0395	0.0268	0.0183	0.0125	0.0086	0.0059	0.0041	0.0028	0.0020	0.0014
43	0.6519	0.4268	0.2805	0.1852	0.1227	0.0816	0.0545	0.0365	0.0246	0.0166	0.0112	0.0076	0.0052	0.0036	0.0025	0.0017	0.0012
44	0.6454	0.4184	0.2724	0.1780	0.1169	0.0770	0.0509	0.0338	0.0226	0.0151	0.0101	0.0068	0.0046	0.0031	0.0021	0.0015	0.0010
45	0.6391	0.4102	0.2644	0.1712	0.1113	0.0727	0.0476	0.0313	0.0207	0.0137	0.0091	0.0061	0.0041	0.0027	0.0019	0.0013	0.0009

Page 1 of 1

PV = $5,000
I = 4 percent
N = ten years
FV = ?

Example 1: Using a future value table, you first find your factor of 4 percent at ten years. The factor number is 1.48, which you then multiply by $5,000, and your future value will be $7,400.

Example 2: You are making $150,000 every year. Using the financial estimate of twelve times your annual income as a retirement goal, your target amount is $1.8 million ($150,000 × 12). If you need $1.8 million to retire in thirty years, and we have 2 percent annual inflation, how much would you need to set aside now in today's dollars?

PV = $1.8 million
I = 2 percent
N = thirty years
FV = ?

Using the future value table, you first find your factor or the intersection of 2 percent at thirty years. The factor number is 1.81, so 1.81 × $1.5 million = $3.258 million. This is what you would need in today's dollars to meet your goal.

To determine present value of a future dollar amount, use a present value of a future amount table or a financial calculator to determine how much you must deposit today to have the given amount you want in the future, where,

FV = future value, or the amount in future dollars
I = interest rate, or the compounding rate for each period
N = number of periods of compounding, usually in years
PV = present value or the amount in today's dollars

Example 1: You would like to make a down payment of $60,000 on a dental office or home in the next seven years. You expect an interest rate of 4 percent. How much would you need to deposit in today's dollars to have $60,000 in seven years?

FV = $60,000
I = 4 percent
N = seven years
PV = ?

First, find the factor where 4 percent interest and seven years intersect. That factor number would be 0.76. Thus, 0.76 × $60,000 = $45,600. This means in this example you would need to put away $45,600 today to achieve your goal.

An annuity is just a series of regular payments. This is done when purchasing a home or a car. In order to figure out what your payments will be, use an annuity table or a financial calculator. You need to know the following information:

TABLE 2   Present Value of $1

$$PV = \frac{\$1}{(1+i)^n}$$

n/i	1.0%	1.5%	2.0%	2.5%	3.0%	3.5%	4.0%	4.5%	5.0%	5.5%	6.0%	7.0%	8.0%	9.0%	10.0%	11.0%	12.0%	20.0%
1	0.99010	0.98522	0.98039	0.97561	0.97087	0.96618	0.96154	0.95694	0.95238	0.94787	0.94340	0.93458	0.92593	0.91743	0.90909	0.90090	0.89286	0.83333
2	0.98030	0.97066	0.96117	0.95181	0.94260	0.93351	0.92456	0.91573	0.90703	0.89845	0.89000	0.87344	0.85734	0.84168	0.82645	0.81162	0.79719	0.69444
3	0.97059	0.95632	0.94232	0.92860	0.91514	0.90194	0.88900	0.87630	0.86384	0.85161	0.83962	0.81630	0.79383	0.77218	0.75131	0.73119	0.71178	0.57870
4	0.96098	0.94218	0.92385	0.90595	0.88849	0.87144	0.85480	0.83856	0.82270	0.80722	0.79209	0.76290	0.73503	0.70843	0.68301	0.65873	0.63552	0.48225
5	0.95147	0.92826	0.90573	0.88385	0.86261	0.84197	0.82193	0.80245	0.78353	0.76513	0.74726	0.71299	0.68058	0.64993	0.62092	0.59345	0.56743	0.40188
6	0.94205	0.91454	0.88797	0.86230	0.83748	0.81350	0.79031	0.76790	0.74622	0.72525	0.70496	0.66634	0.63017	0.59627	0.56447	0.53464	0.50663	0.33490
7	0.93272	0.90103	0.87056	0.84127	0.81309	0.78599	0.75992	0.73483	0.71068	0.68744	0.66506	0.62275	0.58349	0.54703	0.51316	0.48166	0.45235	0.27908
8	0.92348	0.88771	0.85349	0.82075	0.78941	0.75941	0.73069	0.70319	0.67684	0.65160	0.62741	0.58201	0.54027	0.50187	0.46651	0.43393	0.40388	0.23257
9	0.91434	0.87459	0.83676	0.80073	0.76642	0.73373	0.70259	0.67290	0.64461	0.61763	0.59190	0.54393	0.50025	0.46043	0.42410	0.39092	0.36061	0.19381
10	0.90529	0.86167	0.82035	0.78120	0.74409	0.70892	0.67556	0.64393	0.61391	0.58543	0.55839	0.50835	0.46319	0.42241	0.38554	0.35218	0.32197	0.16151
11	0.89632	0.84893	0.80426	0.76214	0.72242	0.68495	0.64958	0.61620	0.58468	0.55491	0.52679	0.47509	0.42888	0.38753	0.35049	0.31728	0.28748	0.13459
12	0.88745	0.83639	0.78849	0.74356	0.70138	0.66178	0.62460	0.58966	0.55684	0.52598	0.49697	0.44401	0.39711	0.35553	0.31863	0.28584	0.25668	0.11216
13	0.87866	0.82403	0.77303	0.72542	0.68095	0.63940	0.60057	0.56427	0.53032	0.49856	0.46884	0.41496	0.36770	0.32618	0.28966	0.25751	0.22917	0.09346
14	0.86996	0.81185	0.75788	0.70773	0.66112	0.61778	0.57748	0.53997	0.50507	0.47257	0.44230	0.38782	0.34046	0.29925	0.26333	0.23199	0.20462	0.07789
15	0.86135	0.79985	0.74301	0.69047	0.64186	0.59689	0.55526	0.51672	0.48102	0.44793	0.41727	0.36245	0.31524	0.27454	0.23939	0.20900	0.18270	0.06491
16	0.85282	0.78803	0.72845	0.67362	0.62317	0.57671	0.53391	0.49447	0.45811	0.42458	0.39365	0.33873	0.29189	0.25187	0.21763	0.18829	0.16312	0.05409
17	0.84438	0.77639	0.71416	0.65720	0.60502	0.55720	0.51337	0.47318	0.43630	0.40245	0.37136	0.31657	0.27027	0.23107	0.19784	0.16963	0.14564	0.04507
18	0.83602	0.76491	0.70016	0.64117	0.58739	0.53836	0.49363	0.45280	0.41552	0.38147	0.35034	0.29586	0.25025	0.21199	0.17986	0.15282	0.13004	0.03756
19	0.82774	0.75361	0.68643	0.62553	0.57029	0.52016	0.47464	0.43330	0.39573	0.36158	0.33051	0.27651	0.23171	0.19449	0.16351	0.13768	0.11611	0.03130
20	0.81954	0.74247	0.67297	0.61027	0.55368	0.50257	0.45639	0.41464	0.37689	0.34273	0.31180	0.25842	0.21455	0.17843	0.14864	0.12403	0.10367	0.02608
21	0.81143	0.73150	0.65978	0.59539	0.53755	0.48557	0.43883	0.39679	0.35894	0.32486	0.29416	0.24151	0.19866	0.16370	0.13513	0.11174	0.09256	0.02174
24	0.78757	0.69954	0.62172	0.55298	0.49193	0.43796	0.39012	0.34770	0.31007	0.27666	0.24698	0.19715	0.15770	0.12640	0.10153	0.08170	0.06588	0.01258
25	0.77977	0.68921	0.60953	0.53939	0.47763	0.42315	0.37512	0.33273	0.29530	0.26223	0.23300	0.18425	0.14602	0.11597	0.09230	0.07361	0.05882	0.01048
28	0.75684	0.65910	0.57437	0.50088	0.43708	0.38165	0.33348	0.29157	0.25509	0.22332	0.19563	0.15040	0.11591	0.08955	0.06934	0.05382	0.04187	0.00607
29	0.74934	0.64936	0.56311	0.48866	0.42435	0.36875	0.32065	0.27902	0.24295	0.21168	0.18456	0.14056	0.10733	0.08215	0.06304	0.04849	0.03738	0.00506
30	0.74192	0.63976	0.55207	0.47674	0.41199	0.35628	0.30832	0.26700	0.23138	0.20064	0.17411	0.13137	0.09938	0.07537	0.05731	0.04368	0.03338	0.00421
31	0.73458	0.63031	0.54125	0.46511	0.39999	0.34423	0.29646	0.25550	0.22036	0.19018	0.16425	0.12277	0.09202	0.06915	0.05210	0.03935	0.02980	0.00351
40	0.67165	0.55126	0.45289	0.37243	0.30656	0.25257	0.20829	0.17193	0.14205	0.11746	0.09722	0.06678	0.04603	0.03184	0.02209	0.01538	0.01075	0.00068

PV = present value or the amount of the loan
I = interest rate on the loan
N = the number of years on the loan
PMT = amount of the periodic payments

You will now use an annuity table to find the annuity monthly payment (AMP) factor for the loan.

Example 1: You would like to buy a car for $50,000 and plan on putting $5,000 down. Your interest rate is 4 percent. You plan to take out a four-year loan, and you want to know your PMT or monthly payment.

PV = $50,000 – $5,000 = $45,000
I = 4 percent
N = four years
PMT = ?

Find the intersection of four years at an interest rate of 4 percent. The factor number is 22.58. Multiply this number by the number in thousands by twelve months per year: 22.58 × 45 = $1,016.10 per month or $12,193.20 per year.

Terms of a loan can vary significantly, based on how many payments (or number of years) are needed. In general, the quicker you pay a loan off, the more money you save. However, due to cash-flow issues, you may try to get a longer payout period (or more years to pay the debt). In these cases your monthly payments will be lower, but you will be paying the debt off for a longer period of time. For most business loans, such as purchasing a dental practice, I suggest you attempt to structure the loan for between five and ten years, with seven years being ideal in most cases. You must evaluate your cash flow. If the numbers do not allow enough cash flow to make monthly payments to complete the payout within seven years, this may be an indication that you are overpaying for the practice, your other expenses are too high, you're not producing enough income or production, or some combination of issues.

There are other aspects of loans you should be familiar with, such as interest rate. If you elect to get a loan for which the interest rate is not fixed, you may get a lower interest rate, but you will have a higher risk.

The bank may fix the interest rate for some specific period of time, say one to five years, and then the loan becomes a floating loan. It will be tied to the prime rate. Sometimes you can negotiate that the rate can only go a maximum of 2–6 percent in a twelve-month period. To be safe, always fix the rate, if possible, to reduce your risk. An exception to this is if you know you are going to sell an asset soon; then perhaps it makes sense to take the lower interest rate so your cash flow is increased.

You can structure your loan to be interest-only payments. Each month your payments are lower, but you are not putting anything toward principal. In most cases, this is also a bad idea. In the case of a balloon payment, you pay off the entire loan on your last payment, so over the life of the loan, none of your payments are going toward principal. Your payments are lower, so your cash flow should be better, but in the end, you will make one large payment to pay off the balance of the loan.

Evaluate the terms of your loan. Make sure you have no prepayment penalties. What this means is in some cases the bank or lender will write into the loan agreement that you cannot pay off the loan early; if you do, the bank will charge you a penalty. Structure the loan so there is no prepayment penalty. If you do not have a prepayment penalty, pay the amount of the loan twice a month rather than once a month. That is, if the principal and interest is $1,500 per month, pay $750 on the first of the month and $750 on the fifteenth of the month. You will save significant amounts of money and shorten the amount of time and lower payments on your loan.

For some big-ticket items, you must decide whether you want to lease or purchase. How do you decide? I use a simple approach. If the asset I am considering will increase in value over time, I will, in most cases, purchase it, and if the asset will decrease in value over time, I will lease it. With that said, there are several other considerations when deciding whether to lease or buy.

As a dentist, you will likely lease automobiles, office space, and equipment. Let's start with automobiles. You can sell a car you own whenever you want, you can put as many miles on the automobile as you want, and you have an interest rate on the loan based on your credit history. When you lease an automobile, you are financing the vehicle for only a specific period of time. In most cases, the money factor—the amount of interest

KEVIN COUGHLIN DMD, MBA, MAGD

you are paying—is higher than if you purchase the car. You select the number of miles you expect to put on the vehicle every year—usually ten thousand to fifteen thousand—and if you go over that number, you will pay a penalty. You should consider a lease if you want a new car every few years or if you cannot afford the car you want. Leasing the same car provides lower monthly payments; remember, with a lease you are only paying a loan on part of the value of the vehicle not the total price of the vehicle. As far as tax savings are concerned, you will probably have the same deductions and tax advantages whether you purchase or lease. So if you are planning on holding on to your vehicle for a long time—greater than five years—you will be better off with a purchase.

Office space is another opportunity to consider a lease. In these cases the owner of the real estate is the *lessor*, and the individual who leases is the *lessee*. Since most of you reading this are dentists, I recommend longer-term leases. It is not easy for a dentist to pick up and move. In many cases, the lease will be for one, three, five, or seven years, with an option to extend it. You as the lessee have several types of leases to consider. One type is called a gross lease; the tenant or lessee pays the landlord a monthly rent, and the landlord pays for all other costs, such as taxes, insurance, and utilities. A net lease is when the lessee pays the landlord a monthly rent and some additional expenses agreed upon by both parties. A common type of net lease is called a triple-net lease. In this instance, the lessee (tenant) not only pays the landlord rent but also pays for all expenses such as insurance, utilities, and taxes. This type of lease provides the lessor (landlord) the most protection.

When considering office space to lease, try to select a property in which the office spaces are monitored individually so you'll have no argument about whether you're paying too much or too little for utilities such as heat and air conditioning. Most buildings are set up to be monitored individually, so you pay a percentage, based on the square footage of what is being used, whether you are using it or not. In real-estate terms, you will pay an amount each month based on the square footage you are leasing and an additional amount each month called common area maintenance (CAM) charges. You should consider negotiating into your lease, if possible, the ability to sublease; that is, if you have to leave your space for whatever reason or are unable to use your space full-time, you will have the ability to place someone else into the space to reduce your monthly cost.

From a purely financial standpoint, if you are planning to stay in the office space for more than ten years, consider purchasing the property rather than leasing. With a lease, rent tends to increase in cost over time, but a purchase generally will have a fixed interest rate. You should also consider intangible reasons—some individuals just do not want the stress of owning a building and the problems and risks that go with owning and maintaining property. At some point you will consider selling your dental practice, and when that occurs, sometimes leased office space can bring down the overall purchase price. The new owner may have to consider the additional risks of moving in the future and increases in rent and CAM charges over time.

Office equipment can also be leased. You have several types of leases, depending on the equipment. With a property lease, a tenant pays rent for a specific period of time, and the entire lease payment is tax deductible if the property is used for business. You can also have an operating lease or true lease, and this is used for equipment. You pay rent on the equipment; however, at the end of the lease you have the option to purchase the equipment outright. What is important in this type of lease is at the end of the lease, you will have an option to buy back the equipment for 10 percent of the original value. In order for it to be a true operating lease, you must have that option—but not a requirement—and this is important to understand. With this type of lease, you are unable to depreciate the cost of the equipment. However, you can deduct the lease payments. Another type of lease is a financing or capital lease, which is really like borrowing money from a bank. In this case, a leasing company actually will purchase the equipment and then lease it to an individual or a company. In this type of lease, you do not own the equipment, so you can only deduct the interest portion of the lease. At the end of the lease, you do own the equipment and do not have any option to return it. In most cases, you will probably be better off with an operating lease. You should understand that leases do not show up on your credit report or balance sheet, as a loan does. The payment is taken from operating capital. So if you're highly profitable but have high debt structure, sometimes a lease is a good alternative.

CHAPTER 7

UNDERSTANDING YOUR PERSONAL TAXES

T axes are part of life in the United States, and as our government provides more services, it raises money by taxing individuals and companies. Your single largest expense by far will be your taxes. Taxes will be more expensive than your home, car, or education. Because of this, it is critical that you understand your personal tax liability and where and how to try to reduce them. The types of taxes are almost endless. The government may use names other than tax, but make no mistake about it—they are taxes. Some examples of common taxes are federal, state, Social Security, city, sales, property, real estate, death, licenses, excise, gas, inheritance, recording fees, airport departure fees, corporate, entertainment, and hotel. I think you get the message. If we just focus on the basic taxes, consider the following (these numbers may vary by state):

- Federal tax: 28–39 percent
- State tax: 7 percent
- Social Security tax: 7 percent
- Sales tax: 5 percent
- Property tax: 3 percent

Total tax is 50–61 percent, and this does not include the hidden taxes listed above. What this tells you is our country does not have a tax problem per se but a spending problem. Most people I know don't like paying taxes, but what they really dislike is not getting any bang for their buck! Huge amounts of money being spent with very little return on investment and enormous waste are what upset most hardworking Americans. Now enough of my ranting. Let's get back to the issues.

Federal taxes are due on April 15 of the following year. You will pay federal tax on the money you earned, called *earned income*, and you will be taxed on investments you made that make money, called *unearned income*. You will determine your profit and loss from your business, report which are on a schedule C, and then bring that profit or loss to form 1040 for your personal tax. Remember, if you are a corporation or partnership, that entity will also have to file taxes. The IRS considers any money made to be taxable unless the tax code has a waiver. Some of these exemptions are municipal bond income, scholarships or grants, gifts (with restrictions), and some inheritances. When referring to investment income or unearned income, the money is received as capital gains or dividends. Since the IRS considers this unearned, you do not have to pay self-employment tax, Social Security, or Medicare tax. Remember, the IRS considers the value of something to be just like money. If you make someone a denture or give them an implant in exchange for fixing your house, the cost of fixing your house has a value and should be reported, and you should pay taxes on that value. The IRS also states you only pay a tax when you receive the money, so if your stocks go up, you only pay tax on the profit if you sell that stock.

Personal deductions are expenses that are subtracted from income before the amount of tax you owe is calculated. You have personal and business deductions, and for now we will just focus on personal deductions. A personal deduction can only be used if the current tax codes state it is a deduction. It is your job to prove you had a legitimate deduction, not the IRS's job, so it becomes your responsibility to maintain proper records.

There are some standard definitions you should understand when evaluating your personal taxes:

- Gross income is the total income, including all earned and unearned income accumulated in the year.
- Adjustments to income are the adjustments the IRS allows before you calculate your taxable income. Some subtractions that

you may want to consider are contributions to a retirement plan, alimony (but not child support), the cost of moving for a new job, and 50 percent of self-employment tax that you have paid when you are self-employed. The goal is clearly to reduce the dollar amount you will be taxed on. This is called the adjusted gross income (AGI).

- Itemized deductions are standard deductions, and you will use whichever one is greater. A standard deduction can vary depending on your tax status, and you basically have four options: married, single, divorced, or joint. Itemized deductions are just another method to help you reduce your taxable income. Some examples of these personal itemized deductions are medical expenses if in excess of 7.5 percent of your AGI; state and local income taxes; personal property taxes; interest payments on your mortgage; gifts to charity; casualty and theft losses in excess of 10 percent of your AGI; and food, entertainment, or job expenses if in excess of 2 percent of your AGI.

- Personal exemptions can be claimed for yourself, your spouse, or dependents who live with you. Someone over the age of sixty-five who has a disability could provide additional exemptions. Understand that as your income becomes higher the exemptions are phased out, and some wealthier individuals will pay more in taxes.

- Taxable income is the number used to calculate your tax liability—what you owe in taxes. Your goal is to make this number as low as possible. In order to accomplish this, you can decrease your income, increase your adjustments, or increase your deductions and exemptions.

- Tax credits are a one-to-one reduction of your tax liability. A tax credit is better than a deduction. You simply subtract the tax credit from the amount of taxes you owe. Some examples of tax credits that are provided by Congress are child-care and elder-care expenses and foreign taxes that have been paid.

In the United States, we have a progressive tax rate or system for federal taxes. This means the more you make, the more you pay. As your income increases, your federal tax rate increases. Understanding these brackets can help you save significant money. If you are close to going into a higher tax bracket, it might make sense to use a strategy to avoid that higher bracket.

The 1040 is the most basic tax form that all individuals must file with the federal government. This form provides information about your last year's income, allowable deductions, any taxes that you may have already paid or taxes that you may owe. If you are a dentist (or otherwise self-employed), you may find it necessary to provide additional information on a schedule C form. This schedule C form shows profit and loss from your business and details of all income and expenses from running that business. When you are a sole proprietor you fill this form out and transfer the income portion to your 1040 form. Form 4562 is used for depreciation and amortization. It provides information about the age and depreciation status of your equipment.

Schedule A is for the itemized deductions. Remember, you have either standard or itemized and you will elect to take whichever is greater. Form 8283 is for noncash charitable contributions. It should list all donations to charitable organizations, and the total value of the donations is put on your schedule A form. Form 2106 is the form for employee-related business expenses, so if you are an employee you'll list these expenses on this form, and then the total is placed on the schedule A form. Examples of some of these expenses include dues to organizations, auto operating expenses, depreciation, continuing education expenses, and professional books and journals.

Schedule B is where you list interest and dividend income. If this income is greater than $400, it must be listed. The IRS considers this unearned income, so you do not need to pay Medicare or Federal Insurance Contributions Act (FICA) taxes on this type of income.

Schedule D is where you list your capital gains or losses. In most cases, if the asset being sold is less than one year old, it is considered a short-term gain and will be taxed as ordinary income. If the asset has been held for more than one year, then it is considered a long-term gain and is taxed at 28 percent.

Self-employment tax is the amount that a person must pay in for FICA and Medicare. Because you have to pay your own and the matching

Social Security tax, you are able to deduct one half of this amount from your taxable income.

K-1 is a form used if the dental practice files its taxes as a partnership, so in this case each partner has to file a K-1. Remember, a partnership is not a separate taxable entity, so the K-1 is just for your records so you can determine what your profit was from the partnership. You will still fill out the form 1040.

Form 1120 is for corporate tax returns. This is the form a corporation needs to fill out. If you are an employee of that corporation, you will get a W-2 form, which will be entered on the 1040 form.

Now that we've discussed federal taxes, remember that you also have state and local income taxes that will need to be paid, and they can vary considerably. The most important part to remember is you have many additional taxes that need to be addressed and dealt with beyond federal taxes.

The alternative minimum tax is simply a way to make sure everyone has to pay some type of tax. This alternative minimum tax is sometimes called AMT. If you pay by current rules and regulations using all deductions and tax credits and attempt to bring your taxable income to zero the AMT must be calculated, and whichever is higher will be the one used.

If you are a self-employed dentist, you will probably pay estimated taxes because you will not have taxes taken out of your paycheck. Estimated taxes are due on April 15, June 15, September 15, and January 15. If your estimated taxes are too low, you will be forced to pay a penalty and interest. These payments include state and federal taxes, and they will be based on the previous year's taxable income.

Social Security and Medicare are just additional taxes that the federal government places on all earned income only, not unearned income. The Social Security and Medicare taxes are also called Federal Insurance Contributions Act (FICA). They are really two taxes—one for the employer and another for the employee. Anyone who has earned income pays this tax. The employee pays it as Social Security and Medicare, and self-employed individuals as a self-employment tax. The self-employed individual must pay not only his or her portion but match the employee portion also, which amounts to 15.3 percent.

In order to effectively plan a tax strategy, you only can rely on a few options. These options are recharacterizing income, shifting income, postponing taxes, and taking advantages of business expenses. Whenever you can recharacterize your income or make earned income become unearned income, you eliminate the FICA tax immediately. Examples of unearned income would be rent for the office, lease income for equipment, and dividends from your corporation by creating different tax entities. When considering shifting income, you can consider paying family members, who may be in a lower tax bracket. Postponing taxes can occur if you are willing to consider certain types of life insurance annuities and family gifting programs. When you fully understand and control your taxable income, you are on your way to financial freedom.

CHAPTER 8

UNDERSTANDING YOUR BUSINESS TAXES

A business entity such as a C corporation pays taxes on any profits in the business at the end of the year. This type of corporation attempts to eliminate all profits in the corporation in order not to pay double taxes. Some other entities, such as limited liability companies, S corporations, partnerships, and proprietorships, do not pay taxes but allow deductions and income to flow through to the owners.

In order to reduce your business taxes, you must understand what your deductions are and how these deductions can be used. In order for the business to have a deduction, the following terms must be met:

1. The deduction must be ordinary or common to other individuals.
2. The deduction must be necessary in order for you to conduct your business.
3. The deduction must be reasonable in its amount.
4. The deduction must not be personal.
5. The deduction must not be a capital expenditure.
6. The deduction must not relate to tax-exempt income.

When a business makes a purchase of an asset and that asset lasts more than one year, then the asset is considered a capital asset. The IRS has lifetime usefulness standards for these assets. A dental chair has a usefulness of seven years, a dental building has a lifetime usefulness of thirty-nine years, office equipment has a lifetime usefulness of seven years, and leasehold construction is useful for fifteen years. Automobiles have a life expectancy of five years. Most intangible assets have a life span, according to the IRS, of fifteen years.

Depreciation is the word used to describe what is tangible and how much you are able to deduct from your taxes. The form you use is called a 4562 form, and on it you provide the cost of the asset and the IRS lifetime usefulness of the asset. Remember, it is not when the asset is purchased but when the asset is placed in service or use that the deduction becomes available. This depreciation schedule can be done three ways: a straight line, a double-declining balance, or a modified accelerated cost recovery system or (MACRS).

In general, the second and third options will speed up your deduction, which may or may not be beneficial. Because you're a dentist, your income will usually increase over time, so your taxable income will increase. It may be to your advantage to have a greater depreciation down the road when your income is larger, rather than earlier, when your income is less. Remember, land cannot be depreciated; however, the building can be. In many cases, high-tech equipment will be depreciated over a shorter period of time such as five years instead of seven years. Depreciation is a noncash write-off, so it is listed on the income statement, not on a cash-flow statement. This is one reason these two statements may be different.

Some examples of deductible expenses are lease payments, professional supplies, office supplies, stamps, stationery, printing costs, advertising, phone bills, lab bills, malpractice insurance, employee wages and taxes, office insurance, continuing education, mileage for auto (not to and from the office, but from the office to other business interests), interest on loans, depreciation, collections costs, licensure fees, and subscriptions. Nondeductible expenses are principal on loan payments, mileage from office to home and back, cost of land, disability insurance premiums paid, accounts receivable not collected from your patients, and your personal draw.

Tax credits are similar to deductions but even better. A deduction lowers taxable income and in essence lowers taxes; however, a tax credit lowers taxes dollar for dollar. For dentists, the largest and most common tax credit is complying with the Americans with Disabilities Act when equipment is purchased to comply with the act. The maximum tax credit is $5,000. Examples include making your current office wheelchair accessible and your bathrooms handicapped accessible.

Non-income-tax mandates are examples of taxes that are not called taxes. Dentists must comply with the Occupational Safety and Health Administration (OSHA) rules and regulations to stay in business. Make no mistake about it; these are additional expenses borne by the owner or owners.

As an employer you will be mandated to

1. have an EIN or employer identification number for federal and state taxes;
2. have documentation (form I-9) that the employees can work in the United States;
3. withhold income tax from employees' paychecks;
4. withhold FICA from employees' checks (7.65 percent);
5. match this tax, currently another 7.65 percent;
6. report wage and withholding information to employees, currently done on a W-2 form; and
7. report and pay withheld amounts to the government.

Additional costs to employers beyond wages include

1. workers' compensation insurance, purchased through a private insurer to cover job-related accidents and illnesses;
2. State Unemployment Insurance Act (SUTA), a federal program run by the state, usually 1.7–2.7 percent of the first $8,000 in gross wages;
3. Federal Unemployment Insurance Act (FUTA)—beyond FICA, Medicare, and withheld income tax—usually 0.8 percent of the first $7,000 in wages per employee; and
4. matching contribution of 7.65 percent for Social Security and Medicare tax.

In some states, vendors charge a sales tax on all services, including dentistry. Some states require employers to pay a sales tax on certain items purchased outside of the state. Some examples are dental supplies, printing services, subscriptions, and material used from lab bills.

Business entities are taxed differently, depending on how the entity is formed and treated. In a proprietorship, the owner is the business and will pay all taxes under his or her name or employer identification number (EIN). In this case, the employer is not an employee, so the proprietorship does not withhold income taxes. Owners estimate their tax and pay it quarterly to the IRS by filling out a schedule C with their personal 1040 form.

In a partnership, the owner pays and reports employee taxes under the partnership EIN. The owner also pays quarterly taxes.

A corporation is a separate tax entity. The employee pays taxes under the corporation's EIN. The individual is an employee of the corporation. The corporation withholds tax from his or her paycheck. The corporation will have to match Social Security and Medicare taxes for each employee. Each year the corporation will send out a W-2 form, detailing how much the employee earned.

The pass-through entity—S corporation or LLC—is another type of business entity that gets taxed as a partnership. The S corporation or LLC pays no income taxes; however, the profit or loss is divided among the shareholders or members, who report this information on their individual tax returns. If the income is a wage, then the individual withholds and matches FICA. However, if the income is from a dividend, then it is considered unearned and is not subjected to FICA. Single-owner LLCs report taxes as a proprietorship on a schedule C, and multiple-member LLCs report income as a partnership.

Dentists who are owners have some advantages. If you're part of a corporation in which you are an employee, your medical insurance premium is completely deductible for you and your family, and deductible for the corporation also. You may also indirectly deduct disability insurance premiums by having the individuals pay for the premiums themselves, and if the insurance is not used, it is reimbursed. If the owner owns real estate in a separate entity, then he or she can charge the highest reasonable rent, and the income received is considered unearned, so you do not have to pay FICA tax on that income. Business write-offs should be taken through the practice. If you take the deductions on your own rather than through your business, they are called miscellaneous deductions on a schedule A. There is a 2 percent AGI floor for these deductions, so make sure the deductions are run through the business. No floor exists on a schedule C or corporate return.

If you are a dentist and an owner of the practice, you are able to take advantage of several tax laws when you use a professional corporation. A big advantage of incorporation is the tax deductibility of employee benefits. Because you are an employee of the corporation, the medical insurance premiums for you and your family are completely deductible, and they are a tax deduction for the corporation. As I mentioned earlier, disability insurance premiums can also be indirectly deducted by the owner, who pays the disability premiums personally; however, at the end of the year, if the individual has not become disabled, then the corporation reimburses the dentist the cost of the disability premium. If the dentist does become disabled, then he or she would not be reimbursed. That way, the dentist receives tax-free disability benefits.

All businesses can create a cafeteria benefit plan for employees. When incorporated, for example as a C corporation, the dentist is an employee and can participate in the plan. The money that goes into the plan should come from the individual, not the corporation. When this occurs, you are buying benefits pretaxed since the business will not withhold income or payroll taxes. Another advantage of incorporation is setting up other business entities. In the dental field, many times the owner of the corporation also owns the real estate in a separate corporation. In this case, the dental corporation will pay the real estate entity a monthly rental fee to use the space. The IRS considers this income to be unearned, and it is not subjected to FICA or SETA taxes.

In your business tax planning, you should consider maximizing business automobile write-offs. In many cases, dentists take 50–70 percent of their automobile cost as a tax deduction for a business expense. If you own more than one vehicle, I suggest using the most expensive one for business. If you are incorporated, the corporation should own the car, and if unincorporated, you should leave it in the practice's name. You should also consider paying for all operating costs out of the practice to maximize your deductions.

A tax-sheltered retirement plan will benefit most dentists. The key is finding the correct plan for your needs. The simple truth is that most people try to put as much money as possible away for themselves while reducing staff contributions and costs of maintaining the plan. I would suggest you consider two different partners when considering a retirement plan—one who administers the plan and oversees it to make sure you are getting what you want, and a second partner who invests the dollars to provide the greatest return on your investment. Whenever you have an opportunity to put tax-free money away, consider that option seriously. The goal of any solid financial planning is to let you work because you want to, not because you need to.

Most dentists are small-business owners, but you should be aware of the 179 expense election. This will allow purchases up to a certain amount each year as an immediate deduction, which can help with tax planning. In general, if you expect your income to increase dramatically, I suggest you put off deductions for as long as possible. However, if you do not feel your income will be increasing, consider taking your deduction as soon as possible. Do not make a business purchase for the sake of a deduction. You should make a business purchase because you really feel that purchase will help your business. If it won't, don't get lured into it trying to reduce your taxes.

If you are not a practice owner, you do lose many business tax advantages. You may want to consider becoming an independent contractor of some sort, perhaps as a consultant, so you can create your own schedule C in order to deduct legitimate business expenses and reduce your overall tax burden. Remember, as a dentist who is not an owner, you can still deduct your professional expenses on a schedule A under miscellaneous deductions. However, there is a 2 percent floor of AGI (adjusted gross income) that must be met before those deductions can take place. Have the owner of the practice consider paying for some professional expenses and then have their income reduced by that amount. The employee can now receive a 100 percent deduction, and the employer will save on FICA and Medicare taxes because the employee's income will be lower.

In the end, the goal is to maximize legal business write-offs as much as possible and reduce your taxable income because taxes will most likely be your single largest expense. Never cheat—it is not worth it, and your integrity is at stake. In my opinion, individuals who cheat on their taxes cheat in other areas. Does anyone want to see a professional who is a cheat or a liar? I don't think so. Your reputation as a health-care provider is one of your most important assets, so treat it that way. In order to protect that asset, you must keep excellent records in order to

- support items on your tax return;
- aid in tax planning;
- reduce the chances of individuals cheating you or your business;
- identify sources of income;
- track expenses;
- track depreciation; and
- track payments.

CHAPTER 9

PERSONAL AND BUSINESS FINANCIAL STATEMENTS

We will discuss two basic forms: personal forms, which are either personal income statements or personal balance sheets, and corporation forms, which are either corporate income statements, corporate balance sheets, or corporate cash-flow statements.

Let's start with personal income statements. These are statements that are not static; they show an individual's personal cash inflows and outflows. It really is showing you your income minus your expenses. There is generally a time period of one month or one year. The goal of this statement is to see the sources and uses of personal family money. Expenses are grouped by type on the personal income statements. Savings and investments are payments that a person really makes to himself or herself, so they appear on the personal balance sheet, making the statement more positive. Fixed expenses are those that generally cannot be changed over the short term, so most debt service is a fixed expense. Discretionary or variable expenses are those that a person consciously chooses to make. It is important to realize that the difference between income and expenses tells whether a person is living within his or her means. The personal income statement is a good starting point for developing a budget for your personal financial planning. You will learn how you are spending your money and show you patterns of where you are spending your money.

Below is an example of a personal income statement.

BLT Dental PC
Income statement
For the year ended December 31, 2016

Revenues

Sales	$1,200,000.00
Income	$300,000.00
Total revenue	$1,500,000.00

Expenses

Cost of goods sold	$300,000.00
Depreciation expense	$50,000.00
Wage expense	$360,000.00
Rent expense	$120,000.00
Interest expense	$50,000.00
Supply expense	$60,000.00
Utilities expense	$30,000.00
Total expense	$950,000.00
Net income	$550,000.00

A personal balance sheet is a statement of financial position. It shows assets minus liabilities, which equals net worth. It is a snapshot of your financial position at a specific date. What you hope to show on a personal balance sheet is that your net worth is growing over time. You are paying off loans, and as this occurs net worth should increase. In the end, you increase net worth by increasing assets or their value, saving money, and decreasing liabilities by paying down debt.

A personal balance sheet will have assets that are made up of cash, such as checking accounts, saving accounts, money market accounts, and cash in life insurance. You will also have personal assets such as your home, automobiles, and personal property. You will have business assets and finally investments such as stocks, mutual funds, and IRAs. You will then have liabilities that will be made up of short-term liabilities, such as credit card balances, and long-term liabilities, such as auto notes, your mortgage, and student loans. When this is completed, you will subtract your assets from your liabilities and come up with your net worth. Remember, when you're first starting out, you will have few assets other than your education and degree, but you'll have a lot of liabilities, so it is possible to have a negative net worth!

Below is an example of a personal balance sheet.

BLT Dental PC.
Balance sheet
December 31, 2016

Assets

Current assets		
Cash		$300,000
Accounts receivable		$150,000
Prepaid rent		$15,000
Inventory		$10,000
Total current assets		$475,000
Long-term assets		
Leasehold improvements		$100,000
Accumulated depreciation	($10,000)	$90,000
Total long-term assets		$90,000
Total assets		$565,000

Liabilities

Current liabilities	
Accounts payable	$50,000
Accrued expenses	$10,000
Unearned revenue	$5,000
Total current liabilities	$65,000
Long-term liabilities	$100,000
Total liabilities	$165,000

Owner's equity

Owner's equity		
Retained earnings	$100,000	
Common stock	$50,000	
Total owner's equity	$150,000	
Total liabilities and owner's equity	$315,000	

Corporate financial forms are made of a profit-and-loss statement, an income statement, a corporate balance sheet, and a cash-flow statement. The goal of these statements is simply to describe the financial condition of your business, whether it is a corporation, a limited liability company, or a proprietorship.

The profit-and-loss statement, or operating statement, is income minus expenses and shows profit or loss over a given period of time. This type of form details taxable income and expense items, not cash flow. Income statements form the basis for income taxes. If you are a proprietor, you will report this information on a schedule C, which is nothing more than a profit-and-loss statement. Usually the expenses are arranged alphabetically. Another way to show an income statement is in a categorized format form.

Below is an example of income statement in schedule C format.

Corporate profit and loss (income) statement
(Categorized format) for year ending December 31, 2016

Income		
Gross collection	$1,200,000	
Returns and allowances	$5,000	
Net collections		$1,195,000

Expenses		
Staff costs		
Employee benefit program	$10,000	
Pension profit sharing	$70,000	
Wages	$240,000	
Temporary services	$10,000	$330,000

Office space cost		
Depreciation	$10,000	
Rent or lease	$60,000	
Repair or maintenance	$5,000	
Utilities	$10,000	
Office cleaning	$5,000	$90,000
Office expenses		
Insurance	$5,000	
Office expense	$5,000	
Postage	$2,000	$12,000
Marketing expenses		
Advertising	$12,000	$12,000
Bank expenses		
Interest expense	$18,000	
Bank charges	$2,000	$20,000
Variable production		
Expenses		
Dental supplies	$50,000	
Dental lab	$80,000	
Office supplies	$50,000	$180,000
Professional expenses		
Legal and professional	$15,000	
Taxes and licenses	$100,000	$115,000
Owner's expenses		
Auto expense	$15,000	
Meals, travel and entertainment	$15,000	
Dues and publications	$5,000	
Continuing education	$5,000	$40,000
		$799,000
Profit (loss)		$396,000

Remember, the income statement is a tax statement. It shows items such as depreciation, which is not a cash expense but a calculated amount. Loan payments consist of interest and principal. The interest portion is an expense, but the principal is not. Principal is accounted for through depreciation of the asset.

A corporate balance sheet is usually done yearly and allows a business to compare the previous year's financial information with the current year's information. The difference between a corporate balance sheet and a personal balance sheet is that on the corporate balance sheet—there is no net worth. On a corporate balance sheet, it will show the owner's equity in the corporation.

Below is an example of a corporate balance sheet.

Corporation balance sheet
BLT Dental PC
December 31, 2016

Assets
Current assets
Cash accounts	$100,000.00		
Accounts receivable	$150,000.00		
Inventory supplies	$5,000.00		
Prepaid expenses	$5,000.00	$260,000.00	

Long-term assets
Equipment	$250,000.00		
Goodwill	$500,000.00		
Real estate	$350,000.00	$1,100,000.00	$1,360,000.00

Liabilities
Current liabilities
Accounts payable	$60,000.00	$60,000.00

Long-term liabilities
Mortgages	$250,000.00

Other debt	$50,000.00	$300,000.00	$360,000.00
Owners' equity			$1,000,000.00
Total liabilities and owner's equity			$1,360,000.00

Corporate cash-flow statements really show inflows equaling outflows. It is similar to a profit-and-loss statement; however, the difference is this type of statement shows cash receipts and cash disbursements for a specific period of time. Cash flow is important because it shows liquidity or the ability to pay immediate bills. In general, you should have enough cash in your business-checking account for three months of expenses. In most cash-flow statements, you will have cash inflows, which are made up of net practice income, borrowing, and depreciation expenses, and cash outflows, which are made up of net operational costs, doctor's draw, personal expenses paid, loan principals, and payments.

Below is an example of corporate cash flow statement.

BLT Dental PC.
Statement of cash flows
For the year ended December 31, 2016

Cash flows from operating activities

Net income	$300,000
Adjustments to reconcile net income to Net cash provided by operating activities	
Depreciation on fixed assets	$15,000
(Increase) decrease in current assets	
Accounts receivable	($10,000)
Inventory	($50,000)
Prepaid expenses	($10,000)
Increase (decrease) in current liabilities:	
Accounts payable	$50,000
Accrue expenses and unearned revenues	$10,000

Net cash provided by operating activities	$305,000
Cash flows from investing activities	
Purchase of property and equipment	($100,000)
Net cash used in investing activities	($100,000)
Cash flows from financing activities	
Proceeds form line of credit	
Payments on line of credit	$10,000
Proceeds from long-term debt	$100,000
Payment on long-term debt	
Net cash provided (used) in financing activities	$110,000
Net increase (decrease) in cash	$95,000

CHAPTER 10

BUSINESS ENTITIES

When you're deciding what type of business entity to form, you need to think about administrative burdens, cost, tax implications, owner characteristics, and liability protection. In general there are five types of general business entities:

1. Sole proprietorship
2. General partnership
3. Limited partnership
4. Limited liability company (LLC)
5. Corporation

There are four types of business entities for professionals:

1. Sole proprietorship
2. General partnership
3. Professional corporation (PC)
4. Professional limited liability company (PLLC)

A sole proprietorship is the simplest form of business. In this form of business, the owner is the business, so profits and losses are personal. In most cases, the individual running the business is also the owner. Advantages include the following:

1. It is easy and inexpensive to form.
2. You have complete control of the business.
3. There's only one tax to the owner.
4. No separate tax returns are required.
5. Losses flow through to the owner.
6. It is easy to form or dissolve.

Disadvantages include unlimited liability for the owner, and the owner loses fringe benefit deductions.

A proprietorship is not a separate tax entity, so the owner reports all profits and losses on a personal schedule C. This means your tax liability is estimated and must be paid quarterly. You are also responsible for self-employment taxes (SETA), which is similar to Social Security (FICA) and Medicare taxes for the self-employed.

A general partnership is a business entity in which two or more people have a common interest and share of ownership—and profits and losses—of a business. A partnership is a separate legal entity from its owners. There is no limit to the number of partners that you can have, as long as you have at least two.

Advantages include the following:

1. It combines the resources of partners.
2. It is easy and inexpensive to form.
3. Income is taxed once to owners.
4. Losses flow through to owners.

Disadvantages include the following:

1. The owners have unlimited liability.
2. Profits must be shared.
3. Tax returns must be filed.
4. Owners have fewer fringe benefits.

A corporation is another common business entity. A corporation functions as a separate legal entity and has an unlimited life unless shareholders dissolve it. A corporation pays tax on its profits. Individuals may be owners, employees, or both.

Advantages include the following:

1. There is limited shareholder liability.
2. It is a separate entity for tax purposes.

Disadvantages include the following:

1. There is a cost to set up.
2. There is more paperwork.
3. You must comply with federal and state securities laws.
4. You have a risk of double taxation.

You can have different types of corporations. One type is a regular or C corporation and other is an S corporation. The IRS will assume your corporation to be a C corporation unless the owner or owners declare the corporation to be otherwise. Because a C corporation is a separate tax entity, it must pay income tax on any profits. If the C corporation elects to pay dividends, it pays them from after-tax profit. Dividends are taxable income for individuals who receive them, so it is possible that they could get taxed twice, once as a corporation. Remember, professional corporations have a flat rate that is currently at 35 percent, and individuals will also pay (in most states) additional federal and state tax that could be another 45 percent. This is why most professional corporations pay out all corporate profits—to avoid double taxation.

The advantage of a C corporation is full deductibility of employee benefits. The disadvantages of a C corporation are the risk of double taxation on corporate profits and the lack of flow through of losses and tax credits.

Subchapter S corporations follow all the same rules of corporation; however, the owners have elected to be treated like a partnership for tax purposes. The S corporation provides many advantages to the owners. This means all income, losses, credits, and deductions go through the S corporation at the end of the year, and they get carried directly to each individual's personal tax returns. Unlike a C corporation, the S corporation does not pay taxes itself but passes through tax items to the owner. In the S corporation, if dividends are received, they are considered unearned income, and the individual does not pay Social Security or Medicare taxes on the dividend payments.

If you are thinking about selling your professional corporation you are better off having an S corporation rather than a C corporation because the IRS will consider the capital gain in a C corporation, so it will get taxed twice; this would not happen in an S corporation.

Advantages of an S corporation include the following:

1. It provides liability protection.
2. Losses can become personal deductions.
3. Profits are passed through without double taxation.
4. Family income shifting is possible.
5. There is easier accounting and less paperwork than for a C corporation.

Disadvantages of a C corporation include the following:

1. Tax-deductible employee benefits are lost for the owner or owners.
2. You must follow corporate rules.
3. Profits are taxable based on ownership percentages.

Limited Liability Company

This type of entity is even more flexible and combines the best aspects of a corporation and partnership entities. In the dental world, they are referred to as professional limited liability companies (PLLC). Owners in this type of entity are referred to as members and are compensated according to the LLC's operating agreement, which offers different methods of compensation. Additional benefits include the ability to have one or an unlimited number of members. They are easy to establish and can last forever unless dissolved, and there are very few administrative requirements. One disadvantage of a PLLC is that members are generally subject to SETA.

CHAPTER 11

CREATING A BUSINESS PLAN

The difference between an idea and a plan is that a plan is written down. When something is written down, it creates a road map—a document that can be followed—and the chances of success are greatly increased.

A business plan is a document used to project future performance. It usually begins with a general statement and conditions and moves through a more detailed explanation, ending with projections of financial outcomes. Banks, future partners, or investors will be interested in your business plan.

Your written business plan should contain the following parts:

1. Cover sheet
   a. What is the name of the business?
   b. Who is the plan aimed at?
   c. How will individuals get in contact with you?
   d. Who are the principals of the business?
2. Table of contents
   a. Sections and pages that represent the document
   b. All referenced material in the appendix
3. Statement of purpose
   a. What is the business's mission or purpose?
   b. What are you looking for?
   c. Is your business a start-up, buyout, buy-in, or expansion?
   d. What type of entity is the business—proprietorship, partnership, C corp, S corp, or LLC?

    e. How much money will you need?

    f. What will the money be used for?

    g. Why would an investor want to invest in your business?

    h. How do you plan to repay the money you borrow?

4. Description of your community
   a. What are the demographics?
   b. Where did you get this information?
   c. Are there any changes on the horizon?
   d. Is the area growing or shrinking?
   e. What is the economy made up of?
   f. Is it expanding?
   g. Who are the largest employers?
   h. What is the competition?

5. Description of your business
   a. What sets your business apart from other businesses?
   b. What are your short- and long-term strategies?
   c. What are your marketing plans?
   d. What is your location all about—traffic, parking, exposure, and signage?

6. Operations
   a. What are your hours of operation?
   b. What are your credit and collection policies?

7. Personnel
   a. How many and what type of employees will be needed?
   b. What will their duties be?
   c. What will their pay levels be?
   d. How much training will be needed, and what will it cost?

8. Description of applicant
   a. Profession qualifications such as educational background, awards, business experience
   b. Personal information such as your family background—what makes you special?

9. What effects will loans provide?
   a. What are the sources and amounts of funding necessary?
   b. How much money will be needed?
   c. What will you be using the funds for?

    d. How much of the funds will be needed for working capital?

    e. How much of the funds will be needed for personal expenses?

10. Financials (personal)

    a. Personal balance sheet

    b. Personal budget

11. Financials (business)

    a. Last three years of tax returns

    b. Capital expenses over the last five years

    c. Cash-flow estimates by month and by year

    d. Projected income statements over the next five years

12. Appendix

    a. Fee schedule

    b. Appraisal of business

    c. Credit and collection policy

    d. Estimate of any renovation cost

In the end, your business plan is just a plan to show that you have thought out all risks, benefits, alternatives, and options. You are telling the world you are ready and can and will be successful.

CHAPTER 12

UNDERSTANDING THE VALUE OF A DENTAL PRACTICE

If you're practicing dentistry, you probably have considered purchasing or starting a dental practice. There are advantages and disadvantages of purchasing an existing dental practice. Some obvious advantages are instant cash flow, instant staff, and instant patient base. Please keep in mind that each of these advantages also presents some disadvantages.

- After the purchase, will the cash flow be positive or negative?
- Will the staff do what you want?
- Can they be retrained?
- Will the staff be loyal to you and your ideas?
- Will this patient base you purchased stay with you?
- Are they the types of patients you want to provide care for?

Valuation of a dental practice may be necessary in the case of a divorce, death, or dissolution between partners. Remember to consider experts to help you calculate the value of your practice or another individual's practice. My job is to help you understand the process and procedure to help you increase the value of your existing practice or simply not to pay more than necessary for a practice you may be considering for purchase.

The value of a dental practice does not mean the price of a practice; they are different. The value of a dental practice is usually determined by formulas that determine the financial worth of a dental practice. In many cases, the price is determined by emotion; in essence, it may be determined by how eager the seller is to sell and the buyer is to purchase.

As a buyer, you really are considering the income-producing capacity of the practice in question. If the practice has no profit, it has zero value. The physical assets such as supplies, equipment, and real estate may have a value, but the practice does not. This is why production numbers are not really that important. Net income on a tax return is a much better measure of the value. I suggest you do not buy the practice's potential. Only pay for its true value.

Fair market value (FMV), as defined by the IRS, states that it is the price a property would sell for in the open market. It would be the price agreed upon between an eager seller and buyer. The price is determined, for the most part, by each party's motivation to move forward.

Methods of determining a dental practice's valuation can take many forms. You must understand it is not an exact science; however, the following are some methods.

The summation of assets method simply adds up all of the practice's assets and subtracts all of the practice's liabilities. In general, the assets include equipment, supplies, goodwill, financial assets, and real estate, from which you subtract the liabilities. One of the problems with this method is how to value intangible assets. In most cases, the most important intangible asset is goodwill, and the following are some methods to consider in this calculation. You can look at gross production and net income over the last three years of the business. I personally look at the last three years of net collected money on average and apply a percentage of 35–65 percent. The range takes into consideration whether the dentist plans to stay or leave immediately. With regard to the existing staff, how likely is it that they will continue with the practice? Look at trends. Has the practice been growing in terms of the number of new patients and the number and types of procedures? What type of infrastructure is set up in the existing practice? Are reports accurate and up-to-date? Examples of some critical reports that should be run monthly are as follows:

1. How many new patients register per month? Where they are coming from?
2. How many patients are leaving the practice monthly and why?
3. What percentage of total revenue comes from the dental hygiene department and what comes from the dentist? In a typical general dental practice, you would like 25–30 percent of the revenue to come from the hygiene department.
4. The number of active patients who have come into the practice in the last eighteen months. Again, in a general dental practice you need about eighteen hundred active patients to sustain one full-time dentist.
5. How are the accounts receivable? If the receivables are significantly higher than the forty-five-day rule discussed earlier, your financial policies may be too lax. If the number is significantly lower than the forty-five-day rule, you may be losing opportunities because your financial policies are too strict. I suggest you run a report that provides you with a list of patients who have not made any payments on their account in over ninety days. This is telling you that those patients are not happy with the care or service, or there is an issue with their dental insurance. Remember, these patients do not show up for further hygiene appointments.

The profit capitalization method is mostly used to value other types of businesses or other investment opportunities. It really is a method to determine return on investment (ROI). With this method, even though you are a dentist, you may not work in the practice but simply invest your money and have someone else run the practice.

The comparable sales method is the third option to determine value, but it is mostly used to determine the value of real estate. Using this method, you can compare dental practices. With this method, the price of the practice may not be justified by cash flow.

The cash-flow feasibility method allows buyers to determine if they can afford the purchase price and decide if the price the seller is asking is reasonable. In this method, you take revenue minus normal business expenses, taxes, family budget expenses, and retirement plan contributions to determine income available for debt service. This is a very important method, and I suggest you consider it before you agree on a purchase price. If you are not going to have adequate cash flow at the end of the transaction, then perhaps you are overpaying.

Regardless of which of the four methods you use, tax implications in the purchase or selling of a dental practice may be just as important as—or in some cases more important than—fighting over a few dollars on the purchase price or value of the dental practice. The seller must be concerned with capital gains over basis along with depreciation recapture and ordinary income, and the buyer must be concerned with deductibles and depreciation over the useful lifetime of the hard asset and the amortization issues over fifteen years as stated in section 197 of the tax code for assets.

When the seller receives money from the sale of the dental practice, if it is considered ordinary income, then depending on tax bracket, the tax implications for federal tax could be as high as 39 percent plus any state tax. Another option for the seller is a capital gains tax. When you sell a long-term asset for more than it is worth, you will be subject to a capital gains tax. In most instances, long-term capital gains tax is lower than the tax on ordinary income. A capital gain is not considered earned income, so you are not subject to the self-employment tax of Social Security. The buyer would rather have as much money as possible attributed to tangible assets because they depreciate over a short period of time. The buyer will attempt to put as much of the purchase price as possible into supplies, which can be depreciated over one year. Other tangible assets may not be able to be depreciated in a year; they may need to be depreciated over three to seven years. The intangible assets, such as goodwill and restrictive covenants, can only be depreciated over fifteen years. In the end, both parties will agree on a price, and once that is done, the seller will want the majority of the price to be for goodwill that he or she can treat as a capital gain. That money will be taxed at a lower rate and not subjected to self-employment tax or Social Security tax. The buyer will want most of the purchase price to go toward hard assets so he or she can depreciate the cost over one to seven years.

CHAPTER 13

LEADERSHIP

When writing a book about business, the writer would be remiss not to address leadership and management. You must first realize the two are different. Both are important and necessary, but they require different personalities and styles. In order to have a successful business, you must have excellent leadership and management.

I suggest you consider the following ten principles for success. I believe understanding these ten principles, creating an effective plan to organize your life and business, and using them will increase your chances for success.

1. Create a vision for yourself and your business. It should attempt to create your ideal future.
2. Create a code of conduct—not just for yourself but also for your business—that you can live by and are proud of and would want your children to follow.
3. Create processes and procedures that provide relentless communication with your family and your business.
4. Create a financial plan for yourself and your business. This plan should take into account human capital, intellectual capital, and financial capital. Create a financial plan that has balance between work, play, and sharing.

5. Create processes and procedures that constantly raise the bar, not only in your personal life but also in your business. Never stop trying to do better.

6. Create processes and procedures that understand that you are the final decision-maker. Listen and gather information, but remember, in the end you are making the decisions. If they are incorrect, take steps to change them.

7. Create processes and procedures that allow you, your family, and your team members to solicit help and support. Remember, no one knows it all.

8. Demand excellence in yourself and the people around you.

9. Implement and use technology to help you grow, change, and improve.

10. Constantly facilitate positive action steps. Remove the negative, focus on the positive, and continue to move forward.

We can argue whether leadership can be taught or not; however, there is much evidence that successful leaders have certain traits or factors that make them better at leadership. Understanding and implementing the ten principles for success is the first step in understanding leadership.

1. Be motivated. Remember, what motivates one individual may not motivate another. Find the switch for those individuals, and learn how to use it.

2. Be tolerant. You must respect other views, but do not sell yourself out. Try to understand where others are coming from, and realize they most likely don't know where you are coming from.

3. Be willing to trust. You must have trust to create the right environment. Remember the triangle, BLT: you must *believe, like, and trust* the people around you.

4. Have a purpose. You must know what is driving you and your business and what is driving the people around you.

5. Have a vision. It is your ideal future, but it must include core values, and you must realize that some team members may not agree with your vision.

6. Have a positive attitude. When you are positive, your team will feed off that positive energy.
7. Be aware. You must understand your identity and the people around you.
8. Be determined. You will never become a leader without determination. Determination never takes a vacation or gets sick; it is working every day.
9. Be committed. When you say you will do something, you do it. You set an example, and people will respond.
10. Have tenacity. No matter what the challenge, you will never give up.
11. Believe. You have to believe in yourself before others will believe in you.
12. Have faith. You must have faith in yourself and the people around you.
13. Provide inspiration. It is where the ideas come from. Remember, some of the best ideas come from other people.
14. Have self-control. Control yourself. Don't let others control your emotions.
15. Have willpower. It is absolutely necessary. Remember, business—like life—will not always go as planned, so be prepared.
16. Have patience. Success happens over time, not overnight.

Leaders dream and create a desirable future while guiding a person or group. What leaders really do is influence people and events. This is a very important concept to understand. Real leadership is about influence, so think about it.

Managers who are good make leaders look better and help leaders achieve their goals more easily. Managers should consider following an admin scale, which is made up of the following processes:

1. Create a purpose. Your managers will educate and motivate your team on the importance of dental health and treatment.
2. Create a policy. Your managers will create a set of rules or guidelines in order to achieve the purpose. This can be by hiring or training the right people.

3. Create a plan. Your managers will create an outline of the general action steps, using effective communication.

4. Create programs. Your managers will create a series of steps in the correct sequence to carry out the plan or plans, including a review of new and existing dental products and services, and internal and external marketing policies.

5. Create projects. Your managers will create a sequence of steps, with a time frame, to complete a program. These projects should be reviewed weekly or monthly to make sure results are obtained.

6. Create orders. Your managers will create orders or action steps to make sure things get done and determine who does what and when.

7. Create ideal scenes. Your managers will create ideal scenes or visions of how the business should be run, and they should coincide with the practice goals.

8. Create statistics. Your manager will create reports with statistics that compare earlier numbers to present numbers and give a picture of ongoing performance.

9. Create valuable final products (VFPs). Your managers must understand that, as in most businesses, the VFP is a combination of goods and services, and both must be met by high patient satisfaction. Everyone must understand that the final product is a series of subproducts that can make or break your dental practice.

Your leadership and management team are always attempting to provide your patients and your team member's value first. This is simple when something is worth something to someone else. They also must provide one of four types of exchanges. An exchange is a process of offering something valuable in return for some other valuable service or object. You can have four types of exchanges:

1. A criminal exchange when you provide a service that is not necessary or offers no value. Example is doing a crown or root canal when a filling is all that would be necessary.

2. A partial exchange

3. A fair exchange

4. An exchange in abundance

Your goal is to provide an exchange in abundance—not only to your patients, but also to your team members. This is easier said than done. An exchange in abundance is almost unknown, but is the key to success and expansion not just in business but in life too. In essence, this type of exchange simply means you provide better service and a better product than expected. You are providing better value, and when this is done, you create a bond between you and your patients and team members. What is happening is the people around you feel you're giving more than you're getting. In business terms, we refer to these conditions—or scales of conditions from high to low—in the following manner:

1. Power: Your business stats are off the charts, and there is such an abundance of production, even momentary halts or dips cannot pull you down. Enjoy this time. Only two things can happen: it is time to consider selling, or you understand there is only one way to go, and that's downhill.

2. Affluence: Things are going very well. All data in your business looks good. You're moving in the right direction.

3. Normal: Things are moving in a straight line—nothing really bad but nothing really great. This is a very common condition, but if you do not pay attention, it will not take much for you to start going downhill. Remember, nothing is static. It will either improve or start to fail. Complacency is dangerous in business.

4. Emergency: You notice collections and production are not what they should be. Your stats are trending downward, and, if positive action is not taken, your business will fail.

5. Danger: The end of your business is near. Your stats are showing constant decline, managers and leadership are doing other people's jobs, and you are in trouble.

6. Emergency: If positive steps are not taken immediately, your business is done.

7. Nonexistence: You are no longer creating a valuable final product or service. The game is over; your business is finished.

There is a formula to change these negative trends. The first step is to recognize what is happening, take positive action steps, and create positive processes and procedures to influence positive changes in direction. In essence, you must start to promote yourself, your team, and your services. You must change your operating basis, start to economize, prepare to deliver better products and services, and stiffen discipline.

1. Promote: Get going on advertising. Knock on doors, call existing patients, talk up your organization and its team members, and get involved. In many cases, organizations cut advertising, and, in almost all cases, this is the wrong strategy.
2. Produce: Get the dentistry done correctly and efficiently, increase your knowledge and skills, and provide better service. The problem may be you, but you don't recognize it. Take a look in the mirror and the sooner the better.
3. Change your operation: Do not do the same old things the same way, because that is what caused the problem in the first place.
4. Economize: When you start to see improvements, don't go back to the old way. Keep moving forward, and save some money this time around.

Deliver more goods and services. Get out of your comfort zone. In many cases, dentists are allowing tens of thousands of dollars to walk out their doors every day, because they do not want to provide certain services or do not want to take the time to learn. Not only do you have to be ready to deliver more goods and services, but your organization also needs to be ready with the correct infrastructure.

Stiffen discipline not only on yourself, but your entire team too. Everyone must get better and faster. They must understand their jobs better and make fewer errors. Remember, if discipline is not put in, the problem will self-correct on its own with worse results.

In all businesses, the goal is to come up with a winning customer strategy. As business leaders, you are either a believer or achiever. It has been said that 92 percent of all CEOs believe they are providing customer satisfaction; however, only about 8 percent are really achieving it. The 8 percent who achieve it are doing it through a process referred to as the three Ds. The CEO is implementing a process and procedure by designing, delivering, and developing.

Consider designing appropriate segmentation for your patient base and creating a complete patient experience in each segment, from answering the phone and scheduling appointments to creating a comfortable and relaxed office. The goal is a great customer experience from start to finish.

Delivering means every department and every team member must be pulling in the same direction.

Developing means you must reinvent and renew your patient experience over and over, and change must be for the better.

Failure to implement the three Ds correctly will cost you and your business money and time. Take the correct steps, and remember, what is good for your patients will be good for your business. In my experience, I have found that managers feel accountable for improving profits, and I suggest they consider focusing on improving patients' and team members' relationships with their business.

In most businesses your patient base or customer base comprises three categories of people—promoters, detractors, and passives. All businesses want and need more promoters. These individuals like doing business with you, and you enjoy doing business with them. They are the most profitable and least expensive to provide services for. Remember, focus on the promoters, and reward these individuals whether they are patients or team members. Detractors do not usually want to do business with you, and, if the truth be known, you really do not want to do business with them, either. They are expensive to treat, so profits are lower, and they are generally never pleased. This group, whether they are patients or team members, should be removed if you are unable to convert them—the sooner they are removed, the better your business and team will be. The last group is passives. They can go either way. Your job is to move these individuals into the promoter group as soon as possible. By coaching, motivating, and providing excellent service and care, you will win this group over, whether they are patients or team members. In most businesses, only about 20 percent are promoters, 60 percent are passives, and 20 percent are detractors. Recognize these detractors as soon as possible, and do not waste time and energy on them; they will suck the life out of you and your business.

I would like to spend some time on profits. You might not think so, but there are bad profits and good profits. Bad profits occur when they are earned at the expense of customer relationships, when customers feel they have been misled, mistreated, ignored, or coerced. They arise when a company saves money by delivering a lousy customer experience. No profit is worth that type of exchange. When bad profits occur, true growth suffers, reputations are hurt, customers are alienated, and employees become demoralized. You and your company become vulnerable to competition. You have short-term success, but you will fail in the long term.

Good profits occur when your patients are enthusiastic and cooperative. They occur when patients want to come back for more care and services and cannot help but tell others of their great experience. In essence, your patients have become promoters. In business you can calculate the net promoter score (NPS). You simply take the number of promoters and subtract it from the number of detractors; what you're left with is the number of net promoters. Having a practice with a high net promoter score means everything. You will see a high retention rate among your patients, your margins will be higher, annual spending will decrease, cost efficiencies will improve, and your market share will increase.

I suggest that, to measure your success, you implement quality assurance and quality assessment protocols on all processes and procedures. The following is a straightforward example that is helpful and inexpensive. After every appointment, the patient is asked to fill out the following form that is on our financial arrangement sheet. It asks the following questions:

1. Were we on time for your care and treatment?   Yes or No
2. Did we solve your problem?   Yes or No
3. Did we show concern for your problem?   Yes or No
4. Did we explain the fee to you?   Yes or No
5. Would you refer a family member or friend?   Yes or No

All *no* responses must be dealt with right at the point of service. Failure to do so will lead to detractors and lost patients.

CHAPTER 14

DMSOs

What will the future of dentistry look like? Let's be honest. No one really knows. However, I feel we can make several well-informed predictions based on demographics and changes that are occurring right before our eyes.

To start with, group practices are growing, and solo practices are in decline. The reasons are many. Fewer than one-third of graduate dentists are in ownership position after one year. The ADEA states 45.3 percent of new graduates plan to enter practice immediately after graduation, and of this group, 65 percent plan to become an associate in private practice, and 28.3 percent plan to join a corporate group practice. The average graduate of dental school is $220,892 in debt, and 32.1 percent will be over $300,000 in debt. Consider the following: $250,000 debt over seven years at 6 percent interest has a cost of $3652.14 per month. In 2011, the average dental practice was 1800 square feet with three operatories and had a cost of $624,452 and an annual expense of $305,609, for a total of $930,601 for one dentist, two dental assistants, and one part-time dental hygienist. If you work 239 days a year, you will need to collect $3,893.73 per day or $487.10 per hour. What is perhaps most important is that these new graduates lack business, marketing, and communication skills, not to mention comprehensive treatment-planning skills and adequate specialty training. In other words, the cards are stacked against them right out of the gate.

What is being created is a perfect storm for corporate dentistry. My job is not to defend or malign but simply provide information so dentists can make informed decisions. Clearly, what is good for one may not be for another, but please do not underestimate what is coming. I believe it is already here. Work-life balance, interaction with other dentists, flexible schedule, guaranteed salary, less interaction with insurance companies, student debt, and possibly a better and more rewarding exit strategy are all moving dentistry in this direction.

In general terms, corporate dentistry means a variety of practice modalities in which management services at a minimum are provided in a manner that is organizationally distinct from the scope of activities performed by a dentist within his or her own practice. In most cases, practice services are provided via a contract with a third-party organization that is not controlled by the practicing dentist or dentists. The organization is funded by the investments of a for-profit entity that is not directly engaged in the clinical practice of dentistry.

These corporate entities have a variety of different names such as dental service organizations (DSOs), management service organizations (MSOs), or dental management service organizations (DMSOs). These organizations all have similar characteristics but can also differ slightly. In many cases, an equity firm will raise capital for the DSO, and they will often sit on the board of the DSO and receive a share of the profits. They will have a dental director who is not necessarily a dentist and for whom there are no state license requirements. The directors are generally responsible for quality assurance, and they may be employees of or have service agreements with the MSO. Dental ownership usually only means patient records; the DSO owns the dental equipment, supplies, and leases.

You can have DMSOs that do not have outside equity ownership; however, as sizes increase and additional capital is needed, more and more will be backed by equity firms. By definition, an MSO cannot exist without a DSO component, but a DSO can exist without an MSO if the DSO has its own internal management. For those DSOs with outside equity ownership, these equity firms have an interest in maximizing the value of their acquisitions in order to position them for the highest sale price in the future. There is nothing wrong with this. Everyone wants to maximize profit whether they are an individual, a group, or a corporation. The real question is whether there is a conflict of interest. In this model, the equity firm's goal is to take present value of future cash from the business operations to get a multiple of EBITDA for expectation of growth. A point to consider is if, with the drive to increase value, a bubble scenario could be created. The likelihood at the present time, 2016, is slight because these types of DMSOs only make up about 15–20 percent of dental practices, so they have a lot of time for growth and expansion. As more and more of the dental profession consolidates and groups jostle to be the largest, the possibility of overpaying and being unable to give a good ROI to investors increases.

As with any process, procedure, or decision, you should consider using the SWOT analysis. This is where you look at the strength, weakness, opportunities, and threats. When you consider a DMSO, keep in mind some strengths we have already touched on: a possible improvement of life-work balance, steady income, and less stress dealing with day-to-day management. There is also some strength offered to our profession. Several studies show that the unemployed and poor are not receiving adequate dental care. This can be because of cost and or lack of access to care. Arthur Laffer—a member of President Reagan's Economic Policy Advisory Board from 1981 to 1989 and the author of the Laffer Curve associated with supply-side economics—found in Texas in 2012 that DSOs were filling a gap in providing care to the underserved population and were doing it with fewer procedures and at a lower cost. The study was sponsored by Kool Smiles, which at the time was the largest provider of Medicaid in the state, and looked at over twenty five million patient visits. Additional strengths are that competition drives innovation and price containment in all industries, and it could be argued that DMSOs are providing additional competition and could drive fees downward while improving efficiency. The FTC in North Carolina stated that corporate involvement in health-care delivery actually improves coverage and lowers cost, and attempts to slow or stop DMSOs were, in fact, anticompetitive.

A weakness of DMSOs is that you allow someone else to do the worrying. When you become disengaged from the processes and procedures, you are actually giving up control, which may be to your detriment. I have found that a person's personality will be the biggest driving force of success or failure along with type of DMSO and the people who make it up. As in most things you have smart, honest people and smart, honest corporations, and conversely you may also have poorly run corporation and people. If you're truly an entrepreneur, a leader, and a driver, it may be difficult for you to grow and flourish in a DMSO. If your personality moves you to just focus on clinical dentistry, and you have little or no interest in processes and procedures, then it may be an excellent fit. The opportunities in DMSOs can be many if you choose to climb the corporate ladder. Keep in mind that, although opportunities are available, in most cases they will already have business partners. The life span of a DMSO is usually going to be three to seven years; then they will be merged or bought out, and the structure may—and most likely will—change. Sometimes this change is good, and sometimes it is not. Please remember—one thing is for certain: there will be change. Once a certain ROI is met, the equity partners will take their money off the table and move on, and the process will start again. So be prepared. Last, there will be threats. In my opinion, the biggest threat to our profession is that there will be very few solo practices. I will remind those old enough to remember that you no longer see small hardware stores, or markets, or pharmacies; even small mom-and-pop restaurants are few and far between. The other big threat is government regulations. Many states will not allow a nondentist to run a dental office. In fact, when you get through all the contracts and management service agreements, you wonder who is really calling the shots—the DMSO or the dentist. This is for you and the courts to decide. Remember, if it looks like a duck and sounds like a duck, it might just be a duck.

If you are considering a DMSO, you should ask the following questions:

- Who is actually your employer?
- Who will create or edit your treatment plans?
- Who actually owns the dental professional entity and or business entity?
- What type of governance structure is in place?
- Does the business entity have any outside investors, and, if so, how many and who and how much money is involved?
- Is there a manage service agreement in place, and does it comply with state law?

- What are your employer's expectations on productivity and patient flow and/or volume?
- What is your compensation formula, and how is the business entity involved?
- Who owns the leases?
- Who controls patient distribution?
- Who chooses the dental lab?
- Who controls ordering and supplies?
- Who owns patient records? On termination, will you have access?
- How is on-call handled?
- Who makes hiring and firing decisions?
- Will you be compliant with ADA Principles of Ethics and Code of Professional Conduct as well as federal and state laws and regulations?

CHAPTER 15

BUSINESS VERSUS LIFE

In most business books, you will learn about money, profit, and formulas. I would like to end with what is, in my opinion, the most important part of business. It is giving purpose to you and your life. It is about creating something for others to enjoy. It is about providing a service that is needed and can improve the quality of life for others and also for you. Many times, the focus is on customers or patients; however, sometimes we may forget how important our business is to us.

It has been said that real integrity is doing the right thing when nobody is watching. To give real service, you must add something that cannot be bought or measured with money: sincerity and integrity. In the end, if you are going to achieve excellence in big things, you develop the habit in little matters first. Remember, excellence is not an exception: it should be the prevailing attitude. Life should not be measured by the number of breaths we take, it has been said, but by the moments that take our breath away.

There are three stages to life and business. Stage 1 is hard work and creativity. Stage 2 is a period of stasis or maintenance of the status quo. Stage 3 is a period of deterioration or loss. I suggest you stay in stage 1 as long as possible.

Wealth in your life and in your business is really made up of three parts. Part 1 is human capital—our family members, employees, and colleagues. Part 2 is intellectual capital—our street smarts, experiences and knowledge. Part 3 is financial capital—what's in our hand, what's in our pockets, and what's in our hearts and minds. Always remember that the most important capital is human capital. If you always put that first, you will always be on the right track. Enjoy the ride. It is a great trip.

WORKS CONSULTED

Collins, Jim. *Good to Great.* Harper Collins Publishers Inc., 10 East 53rd Street, New York, NY 10022 copywright 2001

Fleming, John H., and Jim Asplund. *Human Sigma Managing The Employee Customer Encounter.* Published by Gallup Press 1251 Avenue of the Americas 23rd floor New York, NY 10020 Copyright 2007 Gallup, Inc.

Gostick, Adrian, and Chester Elton. *The Orange Revolution: How One Great Team Can Transform an Entire Organization.* Published by Free Press A Division of Simon and Schuster, Inc. 1230 Avenue of the Americas New York, NY 10020, Copyright 2010 by O.C. Tanner Company

Heath, Chip, and Dan Heath. *SWITCH: How to Change Things When Change Is Hard.* Published by Broadway Books New York NY copyright 2010 by Chip Heath and Dan Heath

Hubbard, L. Ron. *Speaking From Experience, Illustrated Solutions to the Business Problems You Face Every Day.* Published by Concept Technologies, Inc. 200 North Maryland Avenue, Suite 101, Glendale, California 91206 Copywright 1996

Maxwell, John C. *The 21 Irrefutable Laws Of Leadership.* Published in Nashville, Tennessee, by Thomas Nelson in 2007

Reichheld, Fred. *The Ultimate Question: Driving Good Profits and True Growth.* Published by Harvard Business School Publishing Corporation 60 Harvard Way, Boston, Massachusetts 02163, copyright 2006 Harvard Business School Publishing Corporation

ACKNOWLEDGMENTS

Taylor L. Coughlin, CPA, my daughter who understands more about business than I do.
Nina Coughlin, who continues to help improve my writing skills.

www.ingramcontent.com/pod-product-compliance
Lightning Source LLC
Chambersburg PA
CBHW071822200526
45169CB00018B/727